GOOGLE ANALYTICS
FOR BEGINNERS

The Complete Guide to Advertising
Analysis

Analize Your PPC Campaigns on Google and Youtube
and Improve Your Business Strategies

John Scaglia

Table of Contents

Chapter One

Google Analytics for Beginners

Google Analytics (GA) is a fantastic site tracking device that estimates your web-based advertising and site viability. GA gives essential information on site traffic, watchwords, most visited pages, patterns, and more to aid your promoting and interchanges arranging. In this early session, we'll feature the principal regions of GA to know and make them straightforward. You'll figure out how to discover where your site guests originate from, what number of clients visit your webpage more than once, how guests see your website, to what extent clients stay, which pages your clients particularly like, and how to utilize your site examination to build visits and transformations.

Google Analytics is an awesome wellspring of information on site traffic, yet an appropriate investigation of Google Analytics can let you know far beyond just how much traffic your site is getting.

You can discover a wide range of data on things like traffic sources, for instance, which locales have alluded traffic through to your webpage, which of your internet-based life channels are bringing guests straightforwardly to your site, which watchwords are positioning on Google and accordingly are sending you through traffic, etc.

Notwithstanding traffic breakdown, translation of Google Analytics can likewise give you how guests are connecting with your site by providing details regarding key zones, for example, your top substance, which shows the most mainstream pages of your website, new as opposed to returning guests over-determined timeframes giving you a vibe of how clingy your site is and what number of guests return for future visits, the period of time spent on your website, thus significantly more.

When working with customers, we will cross-examine their Google Analytics information to accumulate some critical benchmark data; for example, referral traffic sources, web index produced traffic, social traffic, etc. We likewise investigate the data further to get essential bits of knowledge into site guest practices, for example, levels of commitment, time spent nearby, most visited pages, run-of-the-mill client voyages taken through the site, and the dropout rates on specific pages.

We additionally measure various kinds of traffic to figure out which is progressively significant, for instance, web index traffic when contrasted with web-based life traffic.

There can regularly be a peril with site examination when you take a gander at measurements in seclusion and reach determinations directly dependent on basically only the information; as a result of this, we lead site to stroll through reviews from the point of view of crucial group of spectators' personas, and we would then be able to overlay site investigation information over this which empowers increasingly active decisions about site use.

A model would be the point at which it is suspected that there are some site structure and route issues, for example, content being covered up too far down a page's structure or site route being excessively unpredictable. In this circumstance, Google Analytics information, for example, the in-page examination, can be utilized to increase genuine proof of a portion of these issues by checking details on navigating rates on various catches and components of the page, and from here the doubt can be affirmed, and a suggested arrangement proposed.

Chapter Two

Why You Need Google Analytics

Reasons You Should Use Google Analytics

Google Analytics is one of the most mainstream advanced investigation programming.

It is Google's free web investigation administration that enables you to break down inside and out insight regarding the guests on your site.

It gives significant bits of knowledge that can assist you in shaping the achievement methodology of your business.

Presently, practically every one of the organizations has an online presence through a site. In this manner, it turns out to be significant for you to become familiar with the inward structure of your website to see whether it is achieving its motivation or not.

For this, you have to know the subtleties of what individuals do when they visit your site, to what extent they remain, and the pages they visit on your website.

Independent of whether you are an online business site or an educational blog, you would need to comprehend and contemplate the conduct of your guests to convey better outcomes.

Given underneath are a few reasons why you should use Google Analytics to show signs of improvement experiences of your site and the guests.

1. It is free

You've more likely than not heard the maxim that "There is no free lunch." But on account of Google Analytics, it isn't valid.

Google doesn't charge you anything for utilizing Google Analytics. You don't need to pay anything to use this item.

These ways, you can put an excellent measure of spending plan in some other significant assets.

Moreover, it gives you essential data, numbers, and measurements that you have to amplify your site's exhibition for nothing.

2. Programmed accumulation of information

Google Analytics has a component that diminishes the work that is required to put Google Analytics information into Google Docs, Sites, or Spreadsheets.

All you have to do is arrange your Google Analytics record and duplicate an essential bit of code on your site.

This will empower Google Analytics to begin gathering information from your site naturally and make reports as needs are.

You basically need to play out no activity so as to get the information. Google Analytics does practically everything for you. You can even access your reports immediately. This element of Google Analytics spares your work exertion as well as gives you quick access to the reports. With this, you can before long execute methodologies for the better execution of your site.

3. You can create customization reports

A custom report is one that you create.

In Google Analytics, you can choose one of the many reports that Google creates or can even build your own customized report using the drag and drop interface.

You can pick the dimensions and metrics and decide how they should be displayed.

To create a Custom Report:

Step 1: Sign in to Google Analytics

Step 2: Navigate to your view

Step 3: Click Customization and then select Reports from the drop-down menu.

Stage 4: Click Customization > + New Custom Report

Stage 5: Enter a Title

Stage 6: Click + Add a Report Tab (Optional)

Stage 7: Select a report type: Explorer, Flat Table or Map Overlay

Stage 8: Define your measurements and measurements

Stage 9: Click + Filter to constrain the report to explicit measurements (Optional)

Stage 10: Select where the report ought to show up. Utilize the drop-down menu to choose explicit perspectives or select All perspectives related to this record to permit this report on all perspectives you approach.

Stage 11: Click Save

4. Simple joining with different devices and steps

Another surprising component of Google Analytics is that it very well may be effectively coordinated with various tools and measures.

Much the same as all other Google administrations, Google Analytics presents an unmistakable and effectively usable interface. Not just does it work very well in the work area, but also it is impeccably usable on Smartphone and Tablet through its application on the Google Play Store.

Google Analytics additionally has fantastic coordination with Google AdWords.

At the point when you connect AdWords account with Analytics, you are fundamentally adjusting two instruments and empowering them to cooperate.

This joined work will furnish you with significant bits of knowledge that will prompt the accomplishment of your AdWords Campaigns.

Henceforth, you can utilize Google Analytics with every one of your gadgets to effectively actualize information to others, surely understand Google items like Google AdWords and Google Search Console.

5. Capacity to gauge inside site search

The interior webpage uncovers what potential clients are searching for in the wake of landing on your site. It likewise uncovers the zone of development opportunity by revealing the circumstances where the specific situation might be misty or lacking on your site.

Fortunately, Google Analytics enables you to follow the interior site to look with a touch of customization.

With this component of inward webpage search, you would be able to have better bits of knowledge of what individuals are looking for on your site. With these bits of knowledge, you can roll out essential improvements or increments in like manner to improve the exhibition of your website.

You can further roll out significant improvements to your site route and item/administration offers.

6. To comprehend why guests are bobbing off your site

Bob Rate is one of the essential measurements which alludes to the level of guests who leave your website in the wake of visiting just one page.

In addition, it is critical to decrease this rate; however, much as could be expected.

A lot of organizations witness colossal traffic yet not adequate transformations. This implies guests are going to your site; however, they are not finding what they are searching for. This prompts a high bob rate. A high bob rate requires a quick activity to distinguish the explanation for it. In any case, Google Analytics gives a point by point report of the pages that are encountering a high ricochet rate. The explanation behind a high bob rate could be that your site isn't advanced appropriately, or perhaps your presentation page isn't appealing enough for them to join.

Along these lines, with the point by point report on bob rate, you can discover available resources to diminish the bob pace of your site.

7. To know the age, sexual orientation, intrigue, gadget, and area of your group of spectators.

With Google Analytics, you can reveal important information about your crowd to figure out which channels drive the vast majority of the traffic to your site.

The Audience area gives a great deal of data about the individuals who visit your site like their age, sexual orientation, interests, gadgets, and region.

It likewise gives you a piece of information on how the guests were headed to your site.

(I) Age: It is probably the best pointer of where your crowd invests the more significant part of the energy. Knowing the average age of your site group of spectators can assist you with optimizing your site as needs are.

(ii) Gender: The sexual orientation variable encourages you to portray your group of spectators. Crowd's sexual orientation assumes a significant job by the way they impart and connect with on the web.

(iii) Interests: With Google Analytics, you can comprehend the benefits of your group of spectators and can improve your site as per their inclinations.

(iv) Device: Google Analytics additionally gives you perspectives on what sort of gadget they are utilizing. With this data, you can enable your site to get increasingly responsive to different devices.

Not just this, with Google Analytics, you can likewise have a view on which sort of cell phone or tablet your group of spectators makes use of.

(v) Location: Understanding where your clients originate from causes you to figure advertising methodologies as indicated by the physical area of your potential clients.

Geolocation highlight of Google Analytics does not just tell you the nation from where your guests are coming from; however, the city from where they are and even the language they use.

8. To comprehend which social platforms to target

Social platforms are an extraordinary method to drive a great deal of traffic and draw in potential clients.

With Google Analytics, you have the entrance to see what grabs the eye of the clients and afterward place the advertisement likewise.

So as to pick the best stage to publicize to your clients, you have to save a liberal spending plan for web-based life advertisements.

For instance: If you see a limit of your client commitment on Facebook and a significant measure of traffic from Twitter, at that point, as per this information, you can set more spending plans for Facebook and relatively less spending plan on Twitter to gain more clients.

With Google Analytics, you can measure the presentation of all the social stages that you are utilizing. You can likewise check how much of transformation esteem every one of the social steps is bringing, traffic entering from social referrals and what number of clients are discussing you.

9. To comprehend what sort of substance you ought to compose

Content is the lord, and whenever made astoundingly, can assist you with getting much more traffic and potential guests.

The great substance is perhaps an ideal approach to connect with your clients, and this is the motivation behind why such huge numbers of organizations make web journals, infographics, and slide shares that can increase the value of your clients.

Google Analytics encourages you to monitor all the substance that gets perspectives and offers. With this information, you can improve the top saw writes, so they request to the clients in an increasingly productive way.

Google Analytics produces a breakdown of the site visits every one of your blog entries gets.

You can adjust on the top performed blog so as to create more traffic.

10. To check if you are accomplishing objectives

The objectives in Google Analytics causes you to follow how a lot of your business is pushing forward and advancing.

You can likewise appoint various objectives that will assist you with tracking the client's voyage dependent on their activities.

There can be a distinctive sort of objectives, such as making a buy, documenting a lead age structure, buying into bulletins, downloading a digital book.

If another guest lands at your presentation page and finishes the given structure, including the email address. He completed an objective chosen by you. Subsequently, with this data, your site changed over a guest into a client, consequently adding to the achievement of your business.

Chapter Three

Account Setup and Interface

1. Account Setup

Step by step instructions to SET UP A GOOGLE ANALYTICS ACCOUNT

You've propelled a site, however now you have to realize how individuals are utilizing it. You have to respond to significant inquiries like, what number of individuals are visiting the site every day? What themes would they say they are searching for once they show up? How are they arriving, and what amount of time would they say they are spending? Google Analytics can respond to these inquiries and a lot more with the establishment of straightforward code.

Google Analytics is an apparently perpetual wellspring of information and knowledge. Yet, you can't get the advantages until you have it set up appropriately, and in case you're new to advanced advertising, that initial step can appear to be overwhelming.

So we're here to demystify the procedure for apprentices.

In this article, we'll stroll through making a Google Analytics account, adding the code to your site, testing the establishment, offering access to proper partners, and defining up objective following.

Making Your Google Analytics Account

To begin, go to the Google Analytics landing page, where you'll see a connect to pursue a free record. Next, you'll be incited to sign in with a current Google login or make another login. When you've signed in, Google will introduce a screen to start setting up your new Analytics account.

Presently, you'll start characterizing criteria for your record. The Account Name ought to be elevated level to your image, in light of the fact that different properties for different sites that are a piece of your vision could be incorporated here. As a preliminary in Google Analytics record structure, note that a record is the most significant level of association. Inside a file, every property speaks to a solitary following code that will be utilized over a site.

Inside every property, different perspectives can channel various approaches to take a gander at traffic on a similar site. For example, you may make multiple perspectives by subdomain (blog.example.com versus store.example.com) or by district (U.S. traffic versus European traffic).

Next on this page, you'll give your site name, which will, at last, become the property name inside this Google Analytics account. Give the site URL, being sure to utilize the dropdown to indicate if the site is on https://(nonsecure convention) or https://(secure).

Utilize the Industry Category dropdown to indicate what specialty your site fits in. Characterizing this class will enable access to Benchmarking Reports, looking at information against different locales in your industry. At last, describe a period zone, taking note that this will influence how information is associated by the hour and day in your record.

Including Your Tracking Code

When completed with the past advances, select "Get Tracking ID" and acknowledge the administration's understanding that shows up. Next, you'll see your property diagram, where the Tracking ID shows up.

Presently you have to add the following code to your site. In the event that you have advancement aptitudes and can get to your site's source code, include the code piece under "Site Tracking" directly before the end tag in your site format. On the off chance that you work with an engineer to deal with your site, duplicate the code, and send it to them to execute.

Some site content administration stages, for example, Squarespace, incorporate a field where you can embed the Google Analytics ID without contacting code. For a site that runs on WordPress, you can introduce a free Google Analytics for WordPress module.

At last, you can utilize the Google Tag Manager to introduce Analytics. When the Tag Manager code is set up, either by you or by an engineer, you can send Google Analytics and alter further viewpoints, for example, objective and occasion following all through one interface.

Checking Traffic

After the following code is set up, you'll need to guarantee that Google Analytics is really catching and demonstrating traffic from the site. To watch that, visit the website from your very own program and go to the Real-Time area of Analytics. In the event that the code is executed appropriately, you'll see visit(s) showing up there.

You can likewise utilize the free Google Tag Assistant augmentation in Chrome to check the right code establishment.

Offering Access to Team Members

In the wake of setting up a Google Analytics account, you'll need to guarantee that any individual who needs access can see the information. In the event that you work for an organization, colleagues, for example, SEO authorities, PPC pros, and record administrators, may all require to get access to it. On the customer side, an advertising supervisor and CEO may both need to have the option to see the information.

To share records get to, go to the Admin area of Analytics, and select User Management on the file, property, or view level.

In case you're sharing access to all properties contained in a record, utilize the record level. In case you're sharing access to an individual property or view (maybe there are numerous sites set up by area, and specific individuals need access to their own regions), utilize the particular alternatives for those classifications.

Once here, you can enter the email address for the individual you'd like to include. Note, this must be a location appended to a Google account.

Pick between access levels depending on what the individual should have the option to do in the record. In case you're offering access to an assistant, they likely need to take a gander at information and shouldn't need access to alter, so "Read and Analyze" access will do the trick. "Alter" level access will enable a PPC administrator to set up a goal following and connection record with AdWords. "Oversee Users" access should just be given to individuals you can trust with the ability to share or remove get to.

Set Up Conversion Tracking

As a matter of course, Google Analytics will follow what number of individuals are visiting your site, to what extent they're spending there, and what pages they're seeing. Be that as it may, you won't see activities straightforwardly identified with business execution, as a matter of course. Transformation following should be set up so as to follow item deals or lead structure entries. Google Analytics Goals will enable you to track the activities that connect with the business and assist check with returning on speculation for different battles.

In the event that your site conveys a "Thank You" page after a structure accommodation or buy, duplicate the URL for that page and utilize the Goal arrangement interface to follow any visits to that URL as a transformation. For more clarity on this, here are more details:

Tracking Business Goals in Google Analytics

Making an interpretation of BUSINESS GOALS TO ANALYTICS GOALS

Examination objectives are the foundation of noteworthy estimation. Be that as it may, as a business or an organization, how would you arrive? How would you take your business objectives and make an interpretation of them into examination objectives that can be utilized to deliver significant knowledge that improve your business?

This post gives a structure you can use to decipher your organization's business objectives into investigation objectives.

Rundown Your Business Objectives

The initial step to making significant investigation objectives is to recognize the central goals of your business sincerely. Start by making a rundown of your association's elevated level activity things or wanted results. Try not to stress a lot over how you are going to gauge them at the present time. Make a rundown and get everything down on paper. It is anything but an impractical notion to converse with your chief or other individuals on your supervisory group to get their contribution, too. Reveal to them that you are attempting to adjust what the organization tracks in an investigation to the objectives of the business. Request that they recognize what they accept is the three most significant destinations for the market throughout the following six a year.

In the event that you work for an office, and are making estimation objectives for a customer, hold an interior gathering with your colleagues who know about the record and ask them a similar inquiry - "What are this present customer's three most significant business goals for the following six a year?" Once you're sure you're in agreement inside, carry the customer into the dialog and talk legitimately with them. Tell them you are attempting to all the more likably adjust web examination with their particular business goals and get their contribution to what they accept they are. This isn't just an incredible chance to get familiar with your customers, in their very own words, yet to ensure the two gatherings are moving toward the battle with similar targets, you additionally embed your organization as your customer's accomplice in business.

What is a portion of the business destinations you may wind up with after this activity?

- Increment investor esteem.

- Develop an online network.

- Increment income from online deals.

- Develop business from repeat clients.

- Better influence internet based life.

The subsequent stage is to separate these into quantifiable business objectives.

Separate Your Business Objectives into Measurable Goals

Business targets are frequently subjective, similar to "All the more likely influence online networking." Quantifiable objectives are quantifiable, identical to "Increment the Twitter retweets and Facebook likes for our blog content." That is quantifiable on the grounds that we can quantify the number of retweets every month and report on the off chance that it is expanding or diminishing.

To make investigation objectives, we should initially separate subjective business targets into quantifiable objectives. To do that, investigate every business objective and, if essential, rethink it utilizing terms that are quantifiable.

When you have a rundown of quantifiable objectives, survey it, and consider which of the things on the outline can be estimated utilizing web investigation. For instance, "Increment income from online deals" is a decent contender for converting into an investigation objective. Online deals can be estimated with Google Analytics Ecommerce Tracking.

Then again, "Increment investor esteem" is definitely not an incredible applicant. We can't quantify investor esteem with a web examination. In this circumstance, we can separate this objective by posting a few drivers of "investor esteem" that can be estimated utilizing web investigation such as:

- Increment income per online client.

- Decrease the expense of getting new online clients.

- Increment development of week by week online membership information exchanges.

When you have separated the destinations into quantifiable objectives, you should create a last rundown. For our situation, the outline resembles this:

When you have divided the goals into measurable objectives, you should create a final draft. For our case, the rundown resembles this:

1. Increment income per online client.

2. Decrease the expense of gaining new online clients.

3. Increment development of week after week online membership information exchanges.

4. Develop the quantity of week after week, clients interfacing with our blog content (online network).

5. Increment income from online deals.

6. Increment income (develop business) originating from rehash clients.

7. Increment traffic (better influence) from internet-based life.

Make Analytics Goals from your Business Goals

So as to make examination objectives, we have to take a gander at every one of the business objectives and distinguish what part of it is quantifiable utilizing web investigation.

On the off chance that you take a gander at every objective, you will see that there is typically something to quantify, and an activity explicit to the estimation that characterizes the goal. To create the investigation objective, we center first around what is being estimated.

For instance, consider #3, "Increment development of week after week online membership information exchanges. Here, we need to quantify "online membership information exchanges." We will stress over the "increment development" of some portion of this business objective when we take a gander at significant bits of knowledge.

To make the examination objective for "online membership information exchanges," view your site and experience the membership information exchange process. Doubtlessly, there will be a "Thank You" page that you can use for characterizing your objective.

Making an objective from a Thank You page

For instance, when you round out the membership page for the ClickZ pamphlet and click submit, you see this:

At the top of the URL is a Thank You page. On the off chance that you were making the examination objective for estimating memberships to the ClickZ pamphlet, that would be the URL that you used to characterize your purpose.

When you know the URL, go into Google Analytics, under Admin > Goals, and click "+ **NEW GOAL**."

Enter a name for the objective – like "New Subscription" and snap the alternative marked "Goal." That's the sort of intention utilized for a "Thank You" page. At that point, click "The following stage."

On this page, enter the page way of the URL of the Thank You page.

As should be evident on this page, there are some extra alternatives you can exploit when characterizing an objective. You can allocate a worth, and you can make a channel. We won't utilize these alternatives in this talk, yet on the off chance that you are keen on getting familiar with them, see Google's documentation for Setting up, alter, and share Goals.

Imagine a scenario where there is forget about its page.

To an ever-increasing extent, the conventional Thank You page is being supplanted by a window overlay, which doesn't have a committed URL.

You will see the URL landing page. We can't utilize this for our information exchange objective since then every visit to the landing page would enlist as an information exchange.

In this circumstance, you have to utilize either a virtual site hit or an occasion to follow the sign-up. In either case, you have to add the following extraordinary code to your site.

Occasions are typically a superior wagered in light of the fact that they don't falsely swell your online visit include in Google Analytics. However, if you need to make an objective channel, at that point, you should utilize a virtual online visit.

To do this, go to Admin > Goals, just as opposed to choosing a "Goal" type objective, make it an "Occasion" type objective. You will, at that point, see a page where you can enter the class and activity that characterizes the aim.

The Label and Value fields are discretionary and are not intended to be utilized in the meaning of the occasion, so it is better left clear.

Objective Reports

When you have an intention set up in Google Analytics, you can see the standard report for the purpose by opening Conversions > Goals > Overview.

1. Here, you can choose the section (gathering of sessions) to apply to the objective report. We are taking a gander at all the meetings.

2. Here, you can choose which Goal you need to take a gander at in the report.

3. Here, you can decide which metric to see. More often than not, you need to take a gander at either Completions (the absolute number of objective hits); or the Conversion Rate (the level of guests who finished the objective).

4. Here, you can see the general Conversion Rate during the timespan.

Now, we have made an investigation objective and perceived how to get to a report. We should make a stride back and recollect the first business objective for which we made this examination objective

"Increment development of week by week online membership information exchanges."

The report shows us the absolute number of objectives fulfillments every week, except it doesn't generally give any understanding into the business objective, which is the means by which to build them. To accomplish that, we have to consider significant bits of knowledge.

Significant Insights

Prior, we noticed that for a quantifiable business objective, there is typically something to quantify and an ideal activity. For the goal we are thinking about in this model, the perfect event is to expand week by week online memberships.

What we need to find, utilizing examination, is some activity that the business can take to make week after week online membership increment. We would prefer not to speculate it, however, to back it up with information. That is the thing that we mean by exceptional knowledge.

A time-tested way to deal with finding significant bits of knowledge with objectives is to utilize sections. The thought is to search for traffic portions that produce a higher transformation rate than usual, and spotlight on making more traffic from that section.

To choose a fragment, click on the "+ Add Segment" button at the highest point of the report, and select one of the choices. We would take a look at this implicitly fragments for "Paid Traffic" and "Non-Paid" traffic.

The paid Traffic change rate is high, while the Non-Paid Traffic has a lower transformation rate.

Presently, we are beginning to get an exceptional understanding. To build week by week memberships, we can suggest expanding the measure of paid traffic.

Yet, we can improve utilizing portions. We can concentrate on the different kinds of paid traffic and see which is ideal. To do that, you should make propelled sections to segregate your particular wellsprings of paid traffic.

An appropriately configured Google Analytics setup enables you to get a complete picture of how people are interacting with your brand online. Thankfully, the setup procedure is relatively simple, even for those with little to no knowledge of coding. If you haven't yet installed Google Analytics on your site, get on it! Create an account, set it up, and begin watching the visits come in. From there, you can analyze user behaviors, interests, and actions to make better informed, more effective decisions about your digital marketing strategies.

Executing ANALYTICS WITH GOOGLE TAG MANAGER

You realize you could be getting more understanding from Google Analytics, yet adding code to your site to follow transformations and different measurements appear to be an overwhelming undertaking. On account of Google Tag Manager, it doesn't need to be! Google Tag Manager exists to make examination execution simpler, enabling you to include or refresh your site labels without adding your extremely bustling IT or improvement office. A simple procedure implies a more prominent capacity to follow new crusades and to gather the information you need.

This section presents Google Tag Manager and clarifies how it very well may be utilized to facilitate the weight of overseeing the tracking code and get more understanding from Google Analytics.

What are labels, and for what reason do I have to oversee them?

Labels are short bits of JavaScript code that you add to your site to empower Google Analytics to follow guest conduct. At the point when you introduced Google Analytics on your website, you include an essential tag to every one of your pages to follow each visit to a page. You may have utilized a WordPress module to introduce the original Google Analytics tag, or you may have included the essential tag straightforwardly into your site layout, with the goal that it is incorporated into the header of each page.

Including the essential Google Analytics tag to your site permits Google Analytics to follow standard measurements, similar to the number of Users,

Sessions, and Pageviews. However, if you need to follow non-exclusive details, such as mailing list enrollments or preliminary record information exchanges, you have to add custom labels to your site to track this progressively explicit data. Custom labels can be written in JavaScript, utilizing strategies from Google's analytics.js library.

When you start adding custom labels to your site, you have to oversee them. Why? Since, as your site's structure changes, the names should be refreshed to remain synchronized with how your site functions. Also, as promoting efforts change and your necessities for information change, you should include, update, and expel labels as proper.

The disadvantage? Overseeing labels requires developer time and can turn into a bottleneck, hindering the improvement of your site. This bottleneck can likewise impede your capacity to follow new advertising efforts. In the event that the designers can't get the labels actualized in time for your next battle, you won't have the details you have to assess execution.

Google Tag Manager (GTM)

Supports the bottleneck via numerous robotizing parts of the label the executives. GTM likewise empowers non-software engineers to include a significant number of the custom labels expected to track advertising efforts.

Example: Tracking Email Signups

Assume you need to track email information exchanges on your blog. Most information exchange forms nowadays don't have a customary "Thank You" page – so there is no chance to get for the fundamental Google Analytics tag (which tracks pages) to catch this information. Instead, your email information exchange process most likely completes with a modular.

In this circumstance, you have to include a label that will fire a Google Analytics Event to follow the structure accommodation that gathers the email address and adds it to your mailing list.

Incredibly, with GTM, you can do this without composing any code or altering your site. When you have introduced GTM, you can actualize following like this by just designing labels in the GTM UI. The remainder of this section strolls through this procedure, delineating the means for executing the following of the blog information exchange.

Setting up Google Tag Manager

To utilize Google Tag Manager, you have to make a record. Give your record a name, and afterward, give your compartment a name. Your holder will hold every one of the labels that you oversee. The vast majority have one compartment for each site, and it is average to name your holder after your site. Select the "Website pages" kind of compartment, including your space, and snap "Make Account and Container."

Once you click "Create," the interface will provide the codes needed to install GTM on your site. Copy that code into your website template so that it is included on every page.

You'll see two codes, one of which should appear as high as possible within the section, and another which should appear after the opening tag. You may want to get your website developer to help with this part.

Our First Tag: Google Analytics Tracking Code

When you've made a record and embedded the code, you can continue with adding Google Analytics to your site. From the Workspace area that shows up in the wake of setting up your record, select "Include a New Tag."

Start by giving your label a descriptive name (for this situation, "Google Analytics" covers its capacity). Next, click the Tag Configuration segment to pick a Tag Type and select Universal Analytics from the alternatives that show up.

Glue your Google Analytics ID into the Tracking ID field. You can discover your ID inside the Property segment of your record. Keep the "Track Type" as Page view, which ought to be the default choice.

Snap the Triggering segment to figure out where you need the code to show up. As a rule, you'll need to follow each page of your site; thus, you can choose the All Pages alternative. When complete, spare your Tag.

Our Second Tag: A Google Analytics Event

Next, we'll make a label that enables us to trigger a Google Analytics Event when a structure is submitted. To start, we'll have to finish a housekeeping task under the Variables area of Tag Manager. Snap "Design" and check the container by "Structure ID" inside the choices that show up.

In the wake of coming back to the Tags segment, we can make another tag as in the past, by choosing the Universal Analytics Tag Type. We name this tag "GA Event Blog Updates Signup," enter our Tracking ID and select "Occasion" under Track Type.

Occasions are characterized by utilizing Category, Action, Label, and Value. Just the Category and Action are required. Here, we are going to use a Category named "Bulletin," and the Action will be "Membership." We should follow different kinds of enlistments in this class with various labels, as "Take a crack at Webinar." Next, we have to disclose to

GTM what structure accommodation to follow as the Event, by including a Trigger. We click the Triggering segment and select the "+" image to make another Trigger, picking a Trigger Type of Form Submission.

Inside the Trigger choices, we check the cases by Wait for Tags and Check Validation to guarantee that GTM tracks entries precisely. In the field beneath, we'll empower the Trigger for any Page URL containing /blog/.

Presently, we have to advise the label on how to explicitly follow the blog membership structure (there may be different structures on our blog pages). To do this, we have to take a gander at the HTML for the page with the blog accommodation structure on it and locate its one of a kind ID.

Utilizing Chrome, we can right tap on the structure in the Megalytic blog and select "Investigate Element." This will open a sheet in the lower half of the program where we can see the HTML. Searching for the structure component, we know that it has the ID "bulletin information exchange structure." We can utilize this ID in the Firing Rule to follow entries of this structure.

Returning to the Trigger exchange, under the "Fire this trigger when..." segment, select the "Structure ID" alternative, pick "approaches," and enter "pamphlet information exchange structure."

Now, we click Save, and our Google Analytics tag has been made.

Testing Our Tags and Publishing Them

As a matter of course, labels are made in "unpublished" mode. To utilize this tag, we should click "Distribute" in the upper right-hand corner of the Overview screen. Before we do that, in any case, we are going to tap on "Review and Debug" to test our labels.

This puts us into debug mode, and when we open the Megalytic blog, we see a panel at the bottom of the screen that shows which GTM tags are firing. So far, so good! Now, we enter an email address in the upper right corner Blog Updates form and click

"Go" to submit it. As you can see, when we do this, the Blog Updates Signup tag fires.

Terrific! We have successfully implemented tracking of our blog signups using Google Tag Manager. Now, we go back to the Overview screen in GTM, exit from Preview mode, and click "Publish" to publish our tags on the live website.

Hopefully, this example has provided some insight into how you can use Google Tag Manager to implement Google Analytics tracking on your website. The fantastic thing about this approach is that, once GTM is installed, you can perform all kinds of tracking without having to write any JavaScript code.

2. Interface

In the event that you need your site to be effective, at that point, it is significant that you utilize an exhaustive examination instrument like Google Analytics. Dissecting your site's traffic will assist you with seeing how your group of spectators is interfacing with your substance and let you perceive how your website is performing after some time.

The Google Analytics interface is brimming with helpful information and essential bits of knowledge. Be that as it may, from the start, the sheer number of tables and outlines can appear to be overpowering.

To fix that, we will

- Consider the absolute most significant investigation that you should screen

- Talk about how to investigate this information so you can increase a superior comprehension of how your crowd is drawing in with your site

- Spread how to utilize this information to improve your WordPress site and advertising techniques.

The Google Analytics interface clarified

Google Analytics is a well-known free device given by Google. Indeed, 66% of all sites utilizing examination innovation are currently using Google Analytics.

Google Analytics works by recording a site's information and afterward showing it in the top to bottom tables, outlines, and charts. Here you can see the Google Analytics landing page interface.

The Reports menu

This is on the left-hand side of the page and lets you access more in-depth reporting for specific areas:

- **Real-time** – Get to know how your audience is interacting with your website in real-time. Learn where they have come from, what content they are viewing, and much more.

- **Audience** – Learn about your audience. Look at the demographics of your guests, how they engage with your content, and what devices they use to access your site.

- **Acquisition** – Discover where your traffic is coming from, how people are reaching your site, and how each traffic source is behaving on your website.

- **Behavior** – Learn how individuals move and behave when they are on your site. Observe data on page views, bounce rates, time spent on site, and more.

- **Conversions** – Enables you to track specific actions that your visitors take – and how effectively your website gets people to take those actions.

Other essential aspects of the Google Analytics interface include.

- **Search** – Use this function to find reports and help documentation quickly.

- **Customization** – Create your own report dashboard, custom reports, and much more.

- **Discover** – Gain more knowledge on Google Analytics and its suite of tools.

- **Admin** – Log into your Google Analytics account, alter your settings, and more.

Google Analytics landing page reports: A brisk look

On your landing page, you'll see a fundamental, take a gander at a portion of the more profound information you can discover in the different zones of the Reports menu.

- **Users** – the number of distinct visitors.

- **Sessions** – the number of visits to your site – a user can visit multiple times, so this number will always be higher than Users or be equal.

- **Bounce Rate** – the number of visitors that leave your site without checking a second page.

- **Session Duration** – how long the average visitor uses on your site.

Traffic report

This report gives you a quick picture of where your traffic has originated from. This would then be able to be utilized to help illuminate your promoting procedure.

Crowd reports

The three Audience reports can help educate your substance system. Knowing where most of your group of spectators lives will assist you with limiting and customizing your blog articles. What's more, information on when your group of spectators visits your site will enable you to arrange for when to post new substances.

Conduct report

This report will show your top pages and give you a snappy thought of what substance is performing and which pages aren't.

How about we take a gander at a portion of the more profound reports, presently. Here is a part of the inquiries those reports can reply:

Where is your site traffic originating from?

Understanding where your site traffic is originating from will assist you with developing your group of spectators later on. In a perfect world, you need the traffic to land at your site from various sources, instead of a single traffic stream.

Select **Acquisition** → **Overview** from the left-hand side of the Google Analytics interface. These reports will give you a decent understanding of whether your advertising systems are working.

For instance, on the off chance that you've been concentrating via web-based networking media, you should search for a decent measure of traffic from **Social.**

If 'natural' traffic is low, at that point, you have to invest energy in improving your site's SEO and investigating watchwords for your substance. Or on the other hand, in the event that 'referral' traffic is up, at that point, you will know your push on visitor posting has satisfied.

For more data on where your guests are coming from and how this traffic from each source is drawing in with your site, select **Acquisition → All Traffic → Channels.**

Which pages are connecting with your guests?

To discover how every individual page on your site is performing, select **Behavior → Site Content → All Pages** from the Google Analytics interface.

Here you can;

- Investigate which pages are getting the most elevated number of perspectives

- See standard time spent on each page

- Study which pages your guests are going along with you and leaving you on.

You would be able to use this information to illuminate your substance in the boarding procedure and distribute business as a natural substance that is speaking to your group of spectators.

Bounce rates

On the off chance that your bob rates are high, at that point, you have to take a gander at the pages that are making individuals quickly leave your site. It may be the case that the catchphrases these pages are positioning for are not pertinent to the genuine substance shown. Or then again, it might likewise not be evident to the peruser where to go next on your site after they have completed an article.

Different purposes behind high bob rates can be specialized, as moderate stacking times, or awful convenience on cell phones. When you have made changes to your page's substance, design, or usefulness, screen your ricochet rates after some time to check whether they decline.

It is of equal importance to track exit page data. In a few pages, you will expect to have high exit numbers. For instance, where a sale is made – a 'transaction completed ' or 'thank you' page.

Notwithstanding, other pages may have high exit numbers that you didn't foresee. Compare these pages to different similar ones that have low exit numbers. This will help you comprehend what aspects of these 'high exit' pages need changing.

Leave pages

It is similarly imperative to track leave page information. A few pages, you will hope to have high leave numbers. For instance, where an exchange is finished – a 'thank you' or 'exchange finished' page.

In any case, different pages may have high leave numbers that you didn't anticipate. Contrast these pages with other comparative page types that have low leave numbers. This will assist you in understanding what parts of these 'high leave' pages need evolving.

Who is your audience?

Getting an insight into your audience, how they interact with your website, where they are from, will help you plan properly for their wants. To know what Google Analytics has for you, begin by going to **Audience** → **Overview** from the main menu.

New versus returning guests

It is critical to comprehend the blend of modern and returning guests that your WordPress site gets. Returning guests are your reliable clients. They give you a group of people to whom you can advance your substance, administrations, and items. Notwithstanding, to develop your business, you ought to likewise be continually captivating with new individuals, and driving this new traffic to your site.

On the off chance that your new guest numbers are low, hope to improve your site's SEO, to assist you with positioning admirably in Google. Get occupied via web-based networking media by sharing your substance and contacting a more extensive group of spectators. What's more, consider promoting to get your business' name out there.

Low returning guest numbers imply your crowd doesn't care for your site enough to return. This could be because of poor structure, low-quality substance, troublesome ease of use, or something different. Discover the issues and fix them; generally, this could hurt your business.

What are your top gadgets?

Understanding the innovation utilized by your group of spectators to get to your substance is additionally crucial. Further details on gadgets used can be found under **Audience** → **Mobile** → **Overview**.

On the off chance that versatile utilization is down contrasted with different gadgets, at that point, you may need to take a gander at improving the usefulness of the portable adaptation of your site.

As should be obvious, Google Analytics can be an incredibly successful approach to follow your site's exhibition. By getting comfortable with the Google

Analytics interface, you can comprehend what the information is letting you know and afterward utilize this information to settle on educated choices on the most proficient method to improve your WordPress site.

Chapter Four

Analytical Reports

What is a diagnostic report?

Systematic detailing is a kind of business announcing that is utilized to make decisions. Analytical revealing offers both data and analysis, but they additionally incorporate suggestions. Offering suggestions is the enormous distinction among instructive and scientific announcing.

A logical report is a kind of business report that utilizes subjective and quantitative organization information to break down just as assess a business technique or process while engaging workers to settle on data-driven choices dependent on proof and examination.

While Analytical revealing depends on statistics, historical information and can convey prescient examination of a particular issue, its utilization is likewise spread in breaking down current information in a broad scope of enterprises.

It is an easy to use report device that furnishes you with keen information that you can use to screen the traffic on your site. With Google Analytics, you can monitor who is visiting your website, when they visit, to what extent they remain, and whether they return subsequent to leaving. The following are 15 different ways you can redo Google Analytics to meet your organization's instructive needs.

View information in numerous structures

When surveying information from Google Analytics, you don't need to restrict yourself to essential measurements. You can likewise see information as to courses of events, tables, and pie diagrams. This choice takes into account you needing to break down information in your preferred structure.

Make a custom dashboard

Redoing your dashboards enables you to see the measurements that issue the most to all of you in one spot. Pick which measures you need to see and sort them out such that sounds good to you. Measurements can incorporate the number of sessions, ricochet rate, transformation rates, and then some.

Include custom gadgets

When modifying your dashboards, remember to incorporate custom pies, tables, or course of events gadgets, notwithstanding essential measurements. From the Analytics dashboard, you could have up to 12 devices in each view, except if you have an excellent record.

Utilize more than one dashboard

Utilize separate custom dashboards to screen various kinds of information. For instance, you may utilize one panel for internet-based life traffic, another for specific measurements, and a third for webpage quality/use.

Send dashboard measurements to the email

To monitor how the measures on your dashboards change after some time, send them to your email all the time. As indicated by Online Behavior, Google Analytics enables you to send out dashboards to PDF and timetable them to be messaged at explicit interims.

Google Analytics is a user-friendly analysis device that offers you profound data you can use to monitor your website's traffic. With Google Analytics, you can monitor who visits your site, when they visit, how long they stay, and whether or not they return after leaving. Below are some ways you can customize Google Analytics to reach your company's data needs.

View data in various forms

When observing data from Google Analytics, you don't have to limit yourself to basic metrics. You can also see data in the form of timelines, tables, and pie charts. This option allows you to analyze data in your favorite way.

Create a custom dashboard

Customizing your dashboards enables you to view metrics that are of the most importance. Decide on which metrics you want to see and arrange them in a way that is sensible. Metrics can include the bounce rates, number of sessions, conversion rates, and more.

If you don't feel like making your custom dashboards, you can import an already created one. There are a lot of accessible options, so do your research until you find the right choice for your website.

Import custom reports

As regards custom dashboards, certain types of custom reports are also available for import. If you don't want to make your own reports, import some that have already been developed. According to eConsultancy, you can bring in custom reports for referring sites, SEO, keyword analysis, 404 pages, and more.

Create scheduled reports

As opposed to manually creating reports every time you wish to review data, schedule the creation of custom reports, and receive the results via email.

Adjust date ranges

When viewing any metric or report generated by Google Analytics, the program will display data using a default date range. Adjust this date range to see both short-term and long-term results

Interface Google Analytics to Google AdSense

In the event that you have a Google AdSense account, you can interface it to Google Analytics and produce relevant information. After both of your records are connected, you will have the option to see navigate rates, changes, and the sky is the limit from there.

Screen transformations

Contingent upon your site's motivation, changes may happen when a client makes a buy, pursues a record, or rounds out a structure for more data about an item or administration. Google Analytics enables you to characterize a lot of activities that comprise an "objective" and afterward screen the number of fruitions that happen on the site. Utilize this component to screen changes.

Set different objectives

Notwithstanding checking changes, you can utilize Google Analytics' objective element for different purposes too. For instance, you may set objectives to screen the number of pages every guest sees or the number of guests who download an archive you give.

Attempt new highlights

Google Analytics is continually turning out new highlights to improve client experience. At the point when you see another alternative, play around with it to check whether it's something you can utilize.

Request help

In case you're new to Google Analytics, altering this device for the greatest viability might be testing. Seek counsel from an expert in the event that you feel overpowered.

The distinction between Reporting and Analytics

Important disambiguation between two significant — and altogether different — types of business insight.

In a great deal of business content you read nowadays, "detailing" and "examination" are two words utilized reciprocally to portray the general application and utilization of information — to follow the progressing wellbeing of the organization and to advise basic leadership.

To me, "examination" is a fancier word, with a refined edge that infers applying more mind and procuring more understanding.

Maybe that is the reason numerous individuals in the business have begun utilizing it when really they're alluding to, or are portraying, plain old (yet at the same time crucial and significant!) detailing.

The truth of the matter is that each term compares to two altogether different capacities, which give diverse incentives to your business.

Also, to befuddle the terms is to lose the essential differentiation between estimating your presentation and exploring your exhibition.

Definitions

Detailing is "the way toward sorting out information into educational outlines so as to screen how various territories of a business are performing."

Estimating center measurements and displaying them — regardless of whether in an email, a slide deck, or an online dashboard — falls under this class.

Analytics is "the way toward investigating information and reports so as to remove significant bits of knowledge, which can be utilized to more readily comprehend and improve business execution."

Contrasts in esteem

Detailing gives you data, and examination gives you bits of knowledge. Announcing brings up issues, examination endeavors to answer them.

Both are important, yet toward various purposes.

What's so unique about Analytics?

Analytics clarifies the "why?" and the "so what?"

How? Since it's dynamic — on something beyond a size of time or interim, you ought to have the option to reshape the information to whatever you need. On the off chance that what you see is a lot of standard measurements, at that point, it isn't really a diagnostic appraisal (or an investigation item).

From this dynamic examination concerning the information, you can determine genuine suggestions about your business. Would it be a good idea for you to change your practices to improve your center measurements?

Along these lines, an investigation is likewise exceptional in light of the fact that it's amazingly noteworthy. Actually, it must be followed upon. The estimation of examination is just genuinely conveyed upon your very own development, only in the event that you think of those prescribed following stages and execute them.

Explicit types of Analytics

Analytics can be impromptu sessions or routine profound plunges.

Associates analysis

The associate analysis is an act of breaking down information by gatherings of clients, where all clients in the group share a specific quality. In SaaS, this property is quite often the timeframe when clients pursued the administration — so there is a January 2018 partner containing clients who joined that month, February 2018, etc. From that point, you can perceive how different partners carry on after some time.

In the event that the February 2018 associate's conduct is strikingly not the same as the typical example — suppose the progressing maintenance is much improved — at that point, you can delve into the information further to comprehend the upgraded presentation.

Were there any unique client procurement systems for the long stretch of February?

Maybe another advertising channel pulled in increasingly qualified leads?

Did deals evaluate another pitch that set increasingly sensible client desires?

Companion examination is a typical and routine practice, which frequently carries it into the overlay of revealing. While it's useful in any occasion with any metric, it's a particularly crucial piece of any investigation of beat since it uncovers why, during the client lifecycle, a client is well on the way to drop. Client achievement groups can utilize these bits of knowledge to work proactively and acquire stir.

Division

The division is the act of grafting your information, recognizing gatherings dependent on various characteristics. For instance, you can fragment your client information by industry vertical, to perceive how client conduct varies dependent on what sort of business they are. Or then again, you can fragment your income information by locale to distinguish what regions of the world are most worthwhile and hold the most open door for your business.

The division is, on the one hand, a fundamental idea — and afterward complex on the other. That is on the grounds that you can accomplish such a great deal with it. For a case of how unique and adaptable division can be, look at one of our component refreshes, where we attempt to clarify every one of the manners in which you can join and dice your information.

The follow-up to Analytics

Contributing the time, devices, and workforce in the examination is not just justified, despite all the trouble on the off chance that you, well, take care of business. The genuine meat of analysis lies in utilizing the discoveries to advise functional and strategic components regarding your business. Improving best rehearses, so measurements improve — this is the worth include.

Snappy overview of a subsequent procedure:

- Collect the consequences of the investigation just as likely clarifications for those outcomes.

- Convey discoveries to crucial players. This can incorporate workers at any level. With regards to numbers and execution, straightforwardness is the best approach. It cultivates comprehension of the measurements and of one's effect, purchase in and excitement for new objectives and strategies, and at last, the establishment for an information-driven culture.

- Recognize objectives and the systems you'll change or strategies you'll test.

- Decide an opportunity to check results. Two weeks? 30 days? Make sure to enable enough time for results to show up. Try not to give the craving to move quick a chance to obstruct your capacity to gain based on what you're attempting.

- Play out a similar investigation to evaluate whether the progressions created the expected outcomes.

Most importantly, both announcing and investigation are vital, and both are genuinely significant.

Notwithstanding, they are not something very similar.

Popular expressions regularly get in the tech world, and all of a sudden everybody is utilizing the word 'X' to depict thing 'Y.' Words move importance dependent on how they're marked. I believe that is what's in danger with "revealing" and "investigation." Great scientific endeavors are distorted as detailing, and standard KPI presentations are advertised as examination.

In anything, losing carefulness with language costs us lucidity. In business, on the off chance that we confound terms this way, at that point, we don't obviously observe the capacity we're really performing (or paying for). Because of that, we may likewise pass up on the chances the capacity uncovers.

So I trust this disambiguation has been useful! Please now go forward, hold onto your information, and participate in both announcing and examination to reinforce your group and develop your business.

Chapter Five

Campaign Analyzing

An assortment of strategies and tools enable you to comprehend which parts of your campaign are working, and which areas of the market you reach.

While there is clearly a creative side to building up a decent showcasing effort, progressively, it is additionally turning into a science. The ascent of enormous information has implied that campaigns would now be able to be investigated in detail, with the outcomes educating future technique and spend.

Google Analytics reveals to you the origin of your web traffic, from which social webpage to which web crawler. To embrace a formal crusade investigation, you'll have to use UTM codes.

UTM comprises of a shortcode added as far as possible to a link. It implies that you can tell that somebody is from Twitter, however, whether they tapped on a link in your Tweet or Twitter bio, a paid ad, or direct message.

UTM codes reveal to Google the nitty-gritty story of how traffic gets to your site so that you can dissect it in Google Analytics.

It does this by utilizing a couple of various components:

- Source – The referrer of the traffic: Twitter, Facebook, StumbleUpon.

- Medium – The showcasing vehicle of the traffic: CPC, Social, Standard, email.

- Content – The specific advert that drove the traffic.

- Campaign – The name, the particular promo.

While you have some adaptability in your naming shows, it is essential to be predictable. You can utilize Google's URL Builder or a comparative URL generator to improve the procedure, and as the URLs produced are long, it's a smart thought to use a link shortener to clean up the URL.

By portioning the information along these lines, you can market, promoting ROI as a feature of your campaign examination. You can figure out the cost per lead (CPL) as a significant aspect of this, separating your spend by the absolute number of leads picked up during the campaign.

This UTM manage from Buffer strolls you through how to utilize UTMs in more detail.

What to quantify in a campaign analysis

Look at site analytics

Having set up UTM codes, you can follow where your traffic is coming from, and ascribe traffic to explicit crusades.

You may have a different campaign running simultaneously; however, the UTM codes enable you to follow them exclusively. You can break down whether a specific source is demonstrating to be more compelling than another.

Check email analysis

Your email promoting programming (MailChimp is a prevalent and free choice) ought to have the option to quantify the open space of the messages you convey.

This computation takes the number of messages opened and partitions it by the amount sent, subtracting the ones that skipped. This reveals to you the level of messages that were really opened, out of the considerable number of messages that landed in an inbox.

Click through rates reveal to you what number of the messages that were opened tempted individuals to tap on a link and go to your site. You can compute this by separating the number of customers who got your email by the number of buyers that landed at your site through the email campaign.

You can think about your past endeavors, or if you are beginning, have a go at HubSpot's client benchmark study.

CRM information

Obviously, the ultimate objective of any campaign is driving new business. Check your CRM programming to see what number of new chances, leads, and finished deals came about because of your campaign. You will require this information to figure promoting ROI, as new businesses won will be listed here.

Social Intelligence Using Campaign Analysis

This mix of web traffic, email information, and CRM information will give you a decent comprehension of the number of individuals reached on an online campaign.

Contingent upon your brand, industry, or campaign, this information probably won't recount the full story. Your point may have been to build brand awareness, or you might be a purchaser brand with indirect client relationships – a CPG brand whose items are sold in grocery stores explains.

You might need to see increasingly about the socioeconomics of the shoppers you came to, or how your campaign made individuals feel. Social insight can be utilized for campaign examination to add more detail to the information and include an increasingly human comprehension of the individuals you have come to.

These days any campaign, on the web or offline, will have individuals chatting via social media. There is an assortment of social platform measurements you can gauge that will give you a superior comprehension of what has worked, and which market portions it has worked with.

Amounts of mentions

A straightforward metric that will give you a sign of brand awareness: Has your campaign expanded the measure of discussion around the brand?

Our examination shows that up to 96% of brand discussions occurred outside possessed channels, or with make references that don't label the brand, which means a social knowledge is the best way to get all the discussion around your campaign.

Reach

Reach is the potential number of individuals that the mentions will be seen by. It considers the number of devotees of authors who mention you. If your crusade incorporated a VIP or influencer, they are probably going to produce a lot higher reach.

Engagement

What number of individuals really made a move when seeing your campaign? This can give you a sign of the number of individuals that effectively connected with the campaign, and would be bound to review it, regardless of whether they did not navigate to your site.

News inclusion

Some portion of your campaign investigation will be to see what number of media mentions you gathered and arrange them into various layered distributions.

Social intelligence will ensure you don't miss any mentions, and furthermore make it simple to sort the productions. Mentions are consequently classified by site type, which means you can follow the news report and mentions on the top productions that have secured your campaign.

Voice Share

While you may see an expansion in your number of mentions over the web, you need to benchmark this against your rivals to perceive how you have boosted the share of voice in contrast with them.

Buy aim

You can make complex Boolean questions in a social intelligence device like Brandwatch, which means you can discover occurrences of individuals expressing they expect to purchase your item.

Checking for rises in this sort of language can also give you a sign of the number of individuals who have been in contact with the campaign and plan to make a move yet have not done as such yet.

Emotional Response and Sentiment

You can without much of a stretch screen for positive or adverse reactions to your campaign as a decent social intelligence device will possess sentiment examination inherent.

This can be an overview of clear discernment, and you can classify mentions to see the manner sentiment transforms in connection to the products, brand, or campaign itself.

For a more profound jump, you can take an example of mentions and read through them all. As you go, mark each mention with an emotional reaction. This increasing nitty-gritty methodology can uncover outrage, disappointment, disarray, etc., which robotized examination can't.

Brand affiliations

You can find the characteristics individuals partner with your brand or item by making rules that separate the information in various brand affiliations. Observing these after some time can uncover changing frames of mind and affiliations that your campaigns can impact.

Rules, classes, and labels

There are assortments of ways you can cut up your information. This is one of the most dominant parts of social insight, as you can comprehend the geographic, statistic, psychographic cosmetics of the discussion.

You can utilize this division to see where your campaigns have an effect, and if you are arriving at your objective market.

Utilizing a mix of these techniques can give you an itemized comprehension of your campaign, advising how to repeat the victories and avoiding the disappointments in the following effort.

Analyzing Campaign Performance

Anticipating, making, and conveying a digital campaign is a problematic but amazingly rewarding procedure, mainly once it goes live. Be that as it may, each campaign must sooner or later end, and there is continuously one last step simultaneously: the post-campaign analysis (PCA).

If it is your first time to break down a campaign or you've done a couple yet are confused about how to comprehend the numbers, it isn't that troublesome if you know what you're searching for. Here are the things you ought to examine for on the dashboard of your post-campaign analysis:

Budget returns.

Regardless of whether your campaign gives a return on investment (ROI) indeed relies upon how you're estimating this conversion. A few campaigns will be a lead-in to business cycles that are long (a month and a half or more), and a few campaigns will be just about creating awareness in your objective clients' minds (not explicitly anticipating that they should buy from you without even a second's pause).

Awareness measurements are challenging to measure, as they don't give an unmistakable fiscal ROI without further ado, yet they can frequently be demonstrated down-the-track provided that you ask your clients how and where they discovered you, and incorporate 'banner advertisements' or 'display adverts' in that alternative drop-down.

Keep in mind that experts can exhort you on the best way to spread the campaign's budget ideally. In any case, if you have a clear objective to get results, you ought to consider a €5K market investment.

KPI's

Being perfectly clear about what the brand was hoping to accomplish with the campaign will empower those engaged with the PCA to connect the outcomes with wanted results and understand the information.

As opposed to hanging tight for a significant reveal, it's likewise fitting to incorporate an official summary at the beginning of the report to show whether the campaign expertly met objectives it set out to accomplish. Regardless of whether this is eventually uplifting news or not, it helps make preparations for the correct discussions all through.

Think about your objective, and base your inquiries on that. What was the campaign for? What Key Performance Indicators (KPIs) would be a good idea for you to give the most consideration to, and what's the general point of the campaign? What sort of results would you be content with, and what kind of outcome would you settle with? It's in every case great to have an agreeable benchmark and an uncommon benchmark.

Creative execution

Your campaign or website landing page is probably going to be the center or focus of the campaign, uniting the majority of your creative special assistance suggestions and plan resources for prospects and clients. Having a particular page to guide clients to is recommended, as it enables you to be more focused on campaign messaging, yet to try and get them there, you'll have to do that for the creative on the promotion.

You need to drive engagement and action and measure it with the number of clicks, where individuals waited on the ad, and what their input was once they turned into a client. Was your messaging clear and compact? Was it straightforward? Did it summarize your brand well, and did they feel that it was convincing?

Your visuals and contents ought to be convincing and straightforward, with an unmistakable message. We prescribe refreshing them every now and then.

CPM

Cost per-mile is one of your most essential measurements since it's based on volume — so you ought to use it in your analysis, however much as could reasonably be expected.

While only one out of every odd single one of all those per thousand eyeballs will tap on or create a deal for you, it's a great sign that individuals presently understand your brand, and would remember you again should they see another advertisement — or were at a point where they expected to purchase what you were selling.

You can set the cost underneath another competitive price if a specific length and particular day by day volume of impressions isn't essential to you — however, if you need to be increasingly positive about the measure of traffic got, we suggest setting the CPM cost over the normal.

If the nations inside the system have more appeal, we suggest setting a higher CPM (you can change this relying on the demand). The genuine objective is getting to the sweet spot of paying a reasonable cost for the number of individuals who will see what you need to say.

GEO

Various nations have different conversion rates, and to see the most precise outcomes, you can investigate the traffic by nation base through the Google Analytics dashboard, or another Demand Side Platform (DSP). In light of that outcome, you can improve your campaign accordingly.

Different measurements you'll need to observe are:

- Quality score — the importance of your paid search point of arrival and its quality;

- Impressions — the occasions your advertisements are seen by searchers;

- Normal position — takes note of how your advertisement positions versus different promotions;

- Change rate — what number of individuals who click on your advertisement performs the ideal action on your site.

- Complete traffic — full-scale perspective on how the campaign has directed people to the site;

- Traffic by funnel — traffic to the site fragmented by main campaign channels;

- Bounce rate — the level of guests who leave before performing the ideal action;

- Conversions — a quantifiable proportion of how guests have played out the ideal action;

- Data catch — the nature of information acquired from guests landing at your site.

In case you're making a PCA, we'd likewise prompt that you organize a meeting to talk about the yields of the report so you can exchange ideas and conceptualize ways you may improve your next campaign.

CTR

Your click-through rate (CTR) measures how well your ads and keywords are performing by what numbers of guests really click on the advertisements.

Every advertisement format has its own active visitor clicking percentage. Mobile formats customarily have higher CTR; however, mobile formats could have more miss-clicks compared to desktop, so it's not always a sound correlation. In a perfect world, you'll be trying on both desktop and mobile platforms for an exact perspective.

The nature of your creative has an immediate connection to the CTR rate, which is the reason it is suggested to estimate the viability of your creative and where you can improve. An extraordinary method to quantify this is by using a couple of various innovative varieties and checking for the one that works best. The list of sites from where traffic is coming from likewise can be directly connected to CTR, and for those that are failing to meet expectations, you can turn them off (you can do this from your dashboard if needed).

Eventually, you need to see what numbers of individuals were interested in the campaign by the number of clicks. When they get to your site and landing page, they've basically finished the first significant phase of the funnel, and it is up to you what you do with them next.

Things to Double-Check Before Your Next Campaign

So as to appropriately gather information, there are sure things that you have to set up a specific way. A portion of these contemplations are explicit to your organization and can slant your information if you neglect to do them (or treat them terribly). Others include how you set up your product to accumulate data in any case and can have similarly as disappointing outcomes whenever done inaccurately.

Mark these things off your list, and you will be home free. Neglect to do them, and you're left with off base information (headache included).

To assist you with avoiding a major miss, here are gathered lists of seemingly insignificant details to search for before you plunge into your next analysis.

Has the perfect domain been chosen?

You may have various domains that you have to follow consistently. Possibly you have one for your main site, one for your blog, and another for landing pages. Regardless of how your domains are created, it is essential to ensure that you report on the correct one.

If you are a worldwide organization, you might have domains for various nations or dialects. At the point you do your reports, it tends to be hard to monitor which domain has which objective. To ensure your goals and results align, give close attention to the domain you select every time.

Do you have the perfect time span chosen?

After you have the correct area chosen, you ought to likewise ensure the opportune time frame is selected from while it's natural to give an account of what shows up on the dashboard without checking the time, which could undoubtedly prompt careless errors.

For instance, a large number of us do monthly reports regarding the first day of the following month. By then, your reports have likely moved from the earlier month to the present month. All things considered, you'll need to ensure that you modify the time range to mirror the earlier month that you need to provide reports on. (This standard applies to week's end report as well.)

Furthermore, if you are contrasting the current month's progress with the earlier month, ensure that the exact month is reflected prior to starting your analysis.

Do you have to bar specific sources?

Suppose you own a particular channel of marketing - for example, email or paid marketing, you may need to give an account of one source rather than the majority of your sources in general. When sources are altogether displayed on one page, it tends to be anything but difficult to mess up the numbers from one channel with those from another.

To keep away from any perplexity, I propose filtering your sources to focus on each particular channel in turn.

Has your organization's IP been excluded?

It's viewed as a best practice to consistently monitor the traffic you get to your site's pages. And keeping in mind that you positively need this number to be high, you don't need it to mirror the online views that originate from your partners and workers, as this will skew your information.

For instance, suppose you have ten representatives at your business, and every one of them checks various pages on your site five times each day on average. That implies that they are contributing an extra 50 views daily, 350 views weekly, and up to 1,500 views monthly. That information can totally transform your progress toward your month to month objectives.

Are visitors who aren't in your target territory being tracked?

Only one out of every odd business can market to each nation on the planet. This implies you have to give close consideration to the guests who are in your physical geography.

Suppose your target territory in North America, and you are getting 1,000 visits every month to your site from North America. In any case, you likewise find that you are getting another 1,000 visits per month to your website from Europe. If your reports are visits as 2,000 rather than 1,000, you will skew your information since you can work with and sustain the individuals from North America.

To guarantee that you're providing details regarding the correct audience, investigate the IP, surprisingly going to your site. You would then be able to begin to segment, dependent on individuals, who are in your target territory to abstain from investing energy and assets on the individuals who are most certainly not.

Do you tag specific promotions with UTM parameters?

At the point when you run any campaign, it is imperative to follow how everyone is connecting with your advertising - regardless of whether this happens outside your site. For instance, suppose that you are running an advert on Twitter and Facebook to direct people to your site. A few tools may naturally pail that as social media, leaving you with no sign of which platform produced more traffic.

Enter UTM parameters.

In this circumstance, UTM parameters would fill in as labels/tags that enable you to separate the traffic produced between the two sources.

Did you neglect to put a necessary tracking code on your site?

Before you start getting links to your site anyplace, you have to ensure you have the correct tracking code installed on your website. This will guarantee that you are following traffic going to your website, gathering legitimate lead knowledge about guests going to your website, and turn up insight to assist you with improving the measure of traffic you get to your site.

Contingent upon where you have your site, you might not need to stress over this step. For instance, if your website is facilitated on the HubSpot Marketing Platform, you will consequently have the best possible tracking code on the majority of your pages. Nonetheless, if your website is promoted somewhere else, you should put a tracking code on your pages.

If you have been taking a shot at marketing campaigns that direct people to your site and don't see a rise in traffic, which might be a decent sign that you don't have your tracking code set up appropriately. Without this data, it will be tough if certainly feasible to section your database to convey more customized marketing encounters.

Do you have plans to track offline campaigns?

It might appear to be challenging to follow a disconnected crusade how are you expected to realize what number of individuals went to your expo corner?

Thus, we, at times, put this into the "other" campaign and ponder little on tracking it. In any case, without knowing what number of leads and clients we create from offline campaigns, it winds up hard to apportion resources properly.

Whenever you are going to do a public expo, consider planning how you can track individuals going to your site. This can be as basic as inserting a tracking URL on the majority of the assets you hand out rather than merely using your standard landing page URL. That way, at whatever point anybody visits your site, it will be credited to the public exhibition.

Do you have an unmistakable comprehension of the meaning of your metrics?

Prior to starting your investigation, you have to choose which metrics you need to give an account of. Moreover, you have to know what the metrics really mean and how to translate them. Ordinarily, we report on metrics that we think stands for progress, anyway it's conceivable that they may say something altogether unique.

For instance, Google Analytics will provide details regarding the time somebody spends on your site. And keeping in mind that we regularly compare an extended visit to an intrigued guest, this isn't generally the situation. Despite the fact that you'd like to accept that somebody who has clicked around on a few of your pages is loving what they're seeing, it could likewise imply that they are struggling to discover what they are searching for.

As you examine your metrics, burrow further to comprehend what they mean. It may not generally be what it appears from the outset.

Did you insert a tracking code to all the best possible resources?

Probably the hardest thing for advertisers to recall is to set up your tracking resources before your marketing campaign dispatches. This may incorporate yet isn't restricted to making tracking URLs, putting them over the various platforms, or labeling your bits of contents.

If these errands aren't done early, a portion of your analytics could be gone forever. For instance, if you plan on utilizing a tracking URL on your Facebook post yet forgot, you will pass up every one of the clicks that your guests took to get from Facebook to your site. Should you alter the post and include it in, you will have the option to recover a portion of that. However, you still wouldn't have anything.

Chapter Six

Campaign Tracking

An indispensable segment in understanding the exhibition of a digital advertising campaign is having a legitimate campaign tracking set up. Without it, it's troublesome – if certainly feasible – to gather exact campaign information that will take into account analysis and let improvement happen.

Campaign tracking is a progression of parameters that are affixed to a link that focuses on a given site. The parameters are then connected with every guest who taps the connection. This enables the website to follow the client's conduct identified with any blend of the parameters.

Except the parameters are used effectively, the information that is gathered by the web analytics device may not give the experiences that were relied upon because of powerlessness to precisely break down the information. To see how parameters are applied, we'll use Google Analytics, for instance.

Google Analytics comes with five parameters that can be utilized to frame a campaign tracked URL, which are:

- Source: The site or another referrer where the click comes from.

- Medium: The sort of link clicked. (For example, email, organic, PPC, social, and so forth.).

- Term: The keyword searched for.

- Content: The variant of the advertisement clicked on.

- Crusade: The name of the campaign related to the click.

Every one of these parameters gives a touch of data about how the guest got to the site. At the point when the parameters are assembled, a reasonable picture rises. At the point when the information is then accumulated crosswise over numerous visits, extraordinary bits of knowledge can be gathered about how any blend of parameters impacts business goals.

A complete campaign URL would look like this:

http://www.example.com/?utm_source=myfavorit esite&utm_medium=cpc&utm_term=widget&utm_ content=ad1&utm_campaign=

Importance of Campaign Tracking

Without campaign tracking, it's difficult to track campaigns precisely. If campaigns aren't by and large accurately tracked, there is no real way to know whether a campaign is effective or merely squandering cash.

For instance, if an organization runs a Facebook advertising campaign that drives guests to their site, they would need to know the effect that the campaign had on their characterized business targets. To do this, the organization should have the option to section the paid Facebook traffic that goes to their site by means of the campaign from all other Facebook alluded traffic.

So also, the organization might need to section guests from Facebook who were alluded via links that they themselves posted on the wall of their organization's Facebook page or even guests who went to the site by means of a Facebook application that the organization made.

Without tracking of campaigns, all guests who are alluded from Facebook get lumped into a similar container. Just by using campaign tracking can the organization genuinely comprehend the effect that each Facebook activity has on the business.

Problems with Non-Standardized Campaign Parameters

Starting to utilize campaign tracking over the whole association will give better information altogether, yet there is frequently a significant issue with how campaign parameters are being used all through an organization.

The issue emerges when various individuals utilize various varieties of a similar parameter. This can be represented using the equivalent Facebook model. The individual who is responsible for the Facebook advertisement campaign may utilize "Facebook" as the Source in the campaign tracking. The individual who draws in with fans on the organization's wall may use "Facebook" as the Source, and the individual who included the links in the organization's Facebook application may have utilized "Facebook.com" as the Source.

The outcome is that every one of the sources that were characterized in the campaign tracking will then show up independently in the referral source report in Google Analytics. This makes for muddled tracking and a failure to effectively total over all the Facebook activities.

Getting Clean Campaign Data

The arrangement is to institutionalize the parameters that are accessible for use in campaign tracking URLs. This, in any case, can be troublesome except if you have an apparatus to deal with the parameters that can be utilized in a campaign tracked URL.

You could endeavor to make one utilizing Excel or via Google Docs; however, that may not be a reasonable answer for use over an association. There's additionally another free campaign URL tracking device from Social Snap that enables organizations to institutionalize URL parameters alongside various different highlights to help improve the administration of campaigns and the precision of the subsequent information.

Campaign Analytics for Google Analytics

At the point when you can track your ROI on each dispatch, each email, funnel, and advertisement campaign — you can eliminate the excess and focus more on what's working. "You can utilize these to make sense of how individuals are getting to your site (and what they're doing when they arrive)."

This changes your business from one that invests energy, cash, and assets on systems that appear as though they'll function admirably, to a company that makes intelligent, information-driven choices and realizes what procedures will perform well.

To do only that, you need Google Analytics campaign tracking.

ABCs (or UTMs) of Tracking the Origins of Site Visitors

UTM is short for Urchin Tracking Module, a framework that enables clients to label hyperlinks so as to track where guests came from.

In case you're a Google Analytics client (which you ought to be), you can utilize these to make sense of how individuals are getting to your site (and what they're doing when they arrive).

By including extra content to the end of each hyperlink you share, you can label individuals who click the links (and get to your site) with applicable data about:

- Where they originated from
- What they clicked
- Your plan for them

How about we give a fast overview of the diverse paramount UTM parameters:

107

UTM Source

As a rule, the source depicts where your guests originated from.

It reveals to you the particular spot where the referral lives:

- A site
- Social network
- Name of an email portion

Normal sources include:

- Facebook
- Newsletter
- Twitter
- YouTube
- LinkedIn
- The URLs of websites that allude you traffic

UTM Medium

Medium discloses to you how the guests got to your site.

This is the most elevated level approach to sort information with UTMs and therefore incorporates the broadest classifications. The absolute most normal mediums include:

- Email

- Pay-per-click (PPC)

- Banner promotions

- Direct (which reveals to you they directly composed in your site address)

UTM Content

This depicts the particular banner, advertisement, or email used to share the connection.

It is utilized to figure out the creative working best at distributing content or promoting an offer. This will change uncontrollably by content type, platform, and offer. What's more, there's no standard for terminology.

My recommendation?

Be descriptive so as to recall easily what email or promotion you're discussing.

UTM Campaign

The campaign is like content in that it's an entirely optional field.

Its essential reason for existing is to feature limited time offers or substance dispersion procedures so you can without much of a stretch analyze execution cross-platform and time.

Campaign links ought to be steady over every single, distinctive source and media for some random advancement to guarantee the campaign all in all can without much of a stretch be broken down.

Making appropriately ascribed hyperlinks will set aside some effort to become accustomed to; however, the information it gives will be precious.

To make consistency simple, I prescribe making a brought-together report where you track every one of the hyperlinks you use, making it simple to refer to when you're breaking down later.

Fortunately for you, Google makes assembling these links excessively straightforward! They have a free

UTM manufacturer where you can connect your data and consequently produce a hyperlink.

Then we can see what individuals do when they land on your site. Marginally increasingly mind-boggling, more energizing.

NOTE: Before you can begin selling to your audience, you have to know who your optimal client is, the place they are, and what they will purchase.

Make Goals to See Who's Taking Action

Objectives are an approach to follow the moves individuals make on your site by counting specific behaviors.

What makes objectives extremely helpful isn't only the capacity to state how frequently a move was made, yet to see who made a move. Because of the UTM parameters, you can really do this!

Yet, how about we not put things in the wrong order — we should turn out how to set up an essential objective: going for a Lead Magnet.

Stage 1: Go the Admin Section of Google Analytics

Step 2: Go to the Goals Section

Stage 3: Create a New Goal

Stage 4: Pick "Sign Up" Goal Type: Google offers an assortment of objective formats, which should accommodate your particular needs (however, you can make custom ones also). Since we need to track pick-ins, "Join" ought to be ideal for us.

Stage 5: Name Your Goal, and Select Destination for Goal Type

Step 6: Set Up the Specifics for Your Goal

For Destination, change your standard to "Starts with" and include your Thank You page — that is the place individuals who click end up.

Utilizing "Starts with" guarantees all pick-ins are appropriately credited.

The other method to guarantee that we're following good pick ins and not utterly unplanned Thank You page guests, is to make a channel.

This includes including the URL string of the select in page also (look at the realistic underneath). You'll go Funnel to "ON" and include a stage with the page field, including the URL that goes before your goal page.

Set this progression to "Required," and you've included this standard!

For your URL strings, consistently utilize the content after your space name, not the whole URL — Google definitely knows the root area!

When you're set, confirm your objective to ensure you set it up effectively. At that point, click "Save," and you've assembled your first objective in Google Analytics.

Since we set this objective up, we're not going to have any data to read. Along these lines, how about we survey a more seasoned pipe previously followed goals and perceive how we can utilize these objectives with UTM parameters to get knowledge into our clients.

To take a look at these bits of knowledge, you'll need to visit Conversions > Goals > Overview under the detailing area of Google Analytics.

We'll choose an objective starting from the drop at the top, and afterward, close to the base, and we'll change the subtleties from "Objective Completion Location" to "Source/Medium."

Goals are an incredible method to pick up knowledge into what channels are driving the most visits.

With a tad of ability and a ton of legitimate attribution labeling, Google Analytics campaign tracking can give you some extraordinary experiences.

Since we know the strip down expected to follow achievement and what channels are driving that achievement appropriately — how would we use this?

Like I said before, "Objectives are an extraordinary method to pick up understanding into what channels are creating the most visits."

At the point when you can follow your ROI on each dispatch, each channel, each email, and promotion campaign, you can eliminate the excess and focus on what's working.

Focusing on Your Audience

Making sections is quick and straightforward.

You make a lot of decides that incorporate or bar specific individuals. This enables you to limit your group of spectators to take a gander at a particular subset, similar to individuals who selected in for a Lead Magnet, instead of all site guests.

When you've made your fragment, you can investigate how this subset of guests carried on or, for our situation, who is in the subset.

We should stroll through precisely how you can make your very own fragments.

To start with, click "+ Add Segment," which you can discover under the Audience, Acquisition, Behavior, and Conversion segments.

When you open up the section menu, we will make another fragment.

We have two alternatives for how to make our section.

The most precise is to consolidate Goal Completions with traffic source, which gives you a breakdown of site guests who made the move you need to dissect — for this situation, selecting in for the 10-Minute Social Media Audit — that originated from a particular channel.

If you haven't been utilizing objectives, you can, on the other hand, take a gander at site guests who arrived at the Thank You page for the select in.

This usually is less exact and doesn't work in the event that you direct traffic to the Thank You page from some other source, so the best decision is to utilize objectives.

We should stroll through how to really set this up.

In the first place, we will go to Conditions. This is the place we'll choose objective culminations, or page visits, as one of our group of spectators' creation rules.

In case you're utilizing Goals as your consideration rule, make a condition that incorporates Users who have finished the Goal in excess of multiple times. Yes, Google Analytics wording sure sounds odd now and again.

If instead, you're utilizing page guests, you'll set clients to incorporate page that contains the slug of the URL.

Since you have your condition set, you'll go to Traffic Sources and incorporate the channel you need to concentrate on.

For us, it will be Facebook as the source and PPC as the medium, so we can explicitly perceive how our Facebook PPC advertisements performed.

When in doubt, go for at least 3,000 individuals in your crowd — that guarantees you'll have sensible enough subgroups to place some confidence in your age statistic groupings.

You can explore different avenues regarding less, yet the more chances you have in a classification, the more reliable your information will be.

Since you have your sectioned spectators, let's jump further

Understanding Audience Insights

Presently we're going to make sense of precisely who is selecting in (and who's not), so you can accomplish a more considerable amount of what's working.

Understanding your crowd means driving down promotion costs. Understanding your audience means driving down advertisement expenses, or making sense of better procedures for adapting the leads you're getting! Along these lines, if you're keen on spending less OR making more, you should presumably peruse on.

There are two primary sorts of information we will search for:

- Statistic

- Psychographic

Statistic information portrays what individuals resemble.

For the most part, its measurable subtleties like age and sexual orientation; however, we'll be lumping gadget type and area into this class also.

This data causes you to see precisely who you are talking to and will manage the focusing on you to use in your battles.

Psychographic information instead portrays what individuals like.

It's about advantages, pastimes, and preferences. This talks more to the character of the group of spectators. Psychographic information is most dominant when it's utilized to shape your informing.

We'll be taking a look at a couple of various ways Google Analytics characterizes premiums, incorporating partiality classifications and in-showcase portions. We additionally will include a gauge of the group of spectators' endless riches.

Regularly, the family unit salary is a statistic. But since we're just going to have the option to state whether the group of spectators is in the market for extravagance merchandise, it's less hard information and all the more an approach to get a handle on what they are searching for.

Here's a fast breakdown of the information types:

How about we start with the statistic information — it's straightforward (however yields exceptionally intriguing bits of knowledge).

Demographic Data

We're going to really make custom reports, as opposed to utilizing the real experiences tab. That is on the grounds that we have to ensure we take a gander at Users, not sessions.

Be that as it may, we'll track every one of the information focuses you ordinarily take a gander at in the crowd bits of knowledge tab.

For our statistic reports, we need to check

- Age

- Sex

- Area

- Gadget type

To begin, go to Customization and select "+ New Custom Report."

We're going to construct one report to take a gander at statistic information and one to take a gander at psychographic information. That will make it simple to run these reports for a wide range of a group of spectators sections.

Make four Report tabs, one for Age, Gender, Location, and Device Type.

You'll set the Metric to "Clients" for each of the four of these reports — that is the consistency between them.

For Age, the measurement drill down will be Age, for Gender, it will be Gender, and for Device, it will be the Device Category.

Area is the main weirdo; rather than doing a typical pilgrim view, you'll use guide overlay (which replaces the requirement for a measurement).

Save the report when you're set, and you have an instant demographics report to utilize on numerous occasions.

Psychographic Data

We will make another custom report, this time taking a look at Affinity Categories and In-Market Segments.

This will take precisely the same procedure as before, with the exception that our Dimension Drilldowns will be Affinity Category and In-Market Segment, individually.

Google Analytics Goal

The crucial piece of an advanced estimation and enhancement plan is characterizing your objectives. Miss the point, and you'll set yourself up for debacle!

There is a great deal of Google Analytics objective aides accessible, but most guides clarify what objectives you can set up in Google Analytics and how to do it. Also, this is significant, yet there is much more than that!

I prescribe adopting a key strategy when defining and advancing your objectives.

Make Measurement Plan

It is effortless to make a beeline for Google Analytics and set up a couple of objectives. However, hold up a second.

Before you can set up appropriate objectives, you have to concoct an estimation plan.

Your estimation plan is the establishment of everything that pursues.

1.1 Business Objectives

As an initial step, you have to characterize your business goals.

Start by responding to this inquiry:

"For what reason does your organization exist?"

I will accept Amazon, for instance. Here are a couple of assets tending to Amazon's business goals:

- To turn into the best spot to purchase, find, and discover any item or service accessible on the web. Source

- To be earth's most client-driven organization, to construct a place where individuals can come to learn and find anything they should purchase on the internet. Source

As should be obvious, these are critical, elevated level destinations. Obviously, they need to win more cash, yet consider it. These significant level destinations unquestionably bolster that!

1.2 Strategies and Tactics

After you have set your business goals, you have to think of procedures and strategies that help your business destinations.

Amazon model:

Technique: sell items

Strategy: trade on the web and drive physical store visits and deals

1.3 KPIs

Your KPIs ought to be lined up with your business goals, procedures, and strategies.

For internet business organizations, income and worth related measurements are critical.

The model rundown of KPIs for Amazon:

- KPIs for selling on the web are income, reasonable request esteem, net edge, and so forth.

- KPIs for driving physical store visits are discover store area, print voucher, and so forth.

Peruse this inside and outpost about how to characterize significant KPIs to find out additional.

1.4 Segments

You would like to associate your KPIs with various fragments too. The division has a crucial impact on investigating and upgrading your online business.

Here are several recommendations on where to portion your guests on:

- Showcasing channel

- Geographic area

- New versus returning

- Versatile versus non-portable

- Presentation page

1.5 Targets

It is essential to set focuses on every one of your KPIs. For instance, you need your reasonable request for an incentive to be $100 or higher.

This will guarantee that you take the correct activities to improve your KPIs toward your objectives.

Make Implementation Plan

Your estimation plan and figuring out what you need to track is an extraordinary beginning; however, you are not there yet.

Basically, conveying your Google Analytics following code on the majority of your site pages is likely not adequate.

Imagine a scene in which you need to manage AJAX structures. Estimating these kinds of activities requires the following code alterations:

To put it plainly, you need to make an interpretation of the business needs into a specialized execution plan.

Furthermore, archive the specialized prerequisites to quantify things in the correct manner.

Cheerfully, Google Tag Manager can make the life of advertisers and examiners significantly simpler.

If you need to get familiar with GTM, I prescribe to peruse my 20-advance fledglings manage.

What's more, Jonathan Weber and his group at LunaMetrics have distributed an extraordinary book on GTM and Google Analytics, which is unquestionably worth perusing.

"All the time, specialized code changes are required so as to quantify your business needs in Google Analytics precisely."

Adjust Goals to KPIs

In Google Analytics, you can follow 20 distinct objectives for every view. The purposes are isolated in four diverse objective sets.

It's significant that the objectives that you characterize in Google Analytics are, however, much as could be expected in accordance with your KPIs. In any case, Google Analytics objectives are not equivalent to your KPIs or business targets.

Outer information control may be expected to change your Google Analytics information and objectives into your KPIs.

The Google Analytics API, which we will examine later, can assist you with that.

"Google Analytics objectives are not equivalent to KPIs; however, try to adjust them; however, much as could be expected."

Characterize Macro and Micro Goals

In short:

Full-scale objective: the essential objective or transformation on a site. This could be a deal.

Mini scale objective: an auxiliary objective on a site. This could be a bulletin membership.

It is imperative to set up both full scale and smaller scale objectives on your site.

This will assist you in getting an increasingly comprehensive comprehension of your guests' conduct.

Not every person that visits your site will promptly purchase your items or administrations.

Characterizing both large scale and smaller scale objectives makes it likewise progressively simple for you to pass judgment on the effect of one of your miniaturized scale objectives on principle change on your site.

If you discover that before a buy, many individuals watch an item video, you realize your small scale and full-scale objectives are associated.

This is an extraordinary contribution to further streamlining your online business results.

"Each online business has and ought to characterize large scale and small scale objectives for their site."

Set Up Google Analytics Goals

Google Analytics enables you to characterize 20 objectives for every view, separated into four objective sets. Most presumably, you don't have to set up these numerous objectives in a single view.

You have the choice to either characterize your objectives without anyone else or import them by means of the arrangements exhibition.

Make or import objective in my supposition, and you should always set up your own goals as opposed to bringing in one from another person. It's alright to investigate motivation; however, don't merely duplicate them! Your business is unique, thus ought to be your objectives.

Destination Goals

Stage 1: click on "New Goal."

Presently you can pick what objective you need to make and to which space you need to include it.

Stage 2: fill in a name; pick a real opening ID and objective type Goal data

Step 3: fill in your accurate data.

Google Analytics needs you to fill in several fields: Goal URL

Pick the goal URL of your objective (or application screen name)

Allocate money related incentive to the transformation (non-online business objectives) – discretionary, yet profoundly suggested

Set up a channel for your goal – discretionary

Remember:

Continuously check the "thank you" page in the substance reports or by means of "confirm this objective" alternative.

Stage 1 required impacts on the Google Analytics objective pipe report itself; however, the objective change reports remain the equivalent. As it were, setting stage 1 as needed or not doesn't impact the accurate transformation rate in every single other report with the exception of the pipe report.

Objective qualities give a great deal of extra incentive in revealing what and where to advance.

Notwithstanding goal page objectives, you can characterize three more objective sorts:

- Occasion based objectives (for example for on-page communications)

- Length objectives

- Pages/session objectives

Occasion Goals

Occasion following is the way to follow all sorts of on-page cooperations on your site.

Inside your Google Analytics account, you can set up an occasion-based objective.

For instance, an installed YouTube video on your site.

Occasion Category: YouTube video

Occasion Action: Click the play button

Occasion Label: 10 Google Analytics objective tips

Duration and Session/Pages Goals

Setting duration and session/pages purposes are useful to make setting around your most significant objectives on your site.

Instances of questions you can reply through defining up these other objectives:

- Is there a relationship between time nearby and the transformation rate?

- Do converters visit a more significant number of pages than non-converters?

- What number of pages do individuals visit before they convert?

You are restricted to characterize more prominent than term and session/page objectives.

By and by, don't exclusively concentrate on these objectives when attempting to show signs of improvement in business results.

Why? It doesn't acquire additional cash if guests spend quite a while on your site without making any ideal move!

Closing Remarks

Use objective set 1 for your significant aim of scale and legitimately related objectives. For example, objective 1 is the web-based business thank you page, and objective 2 to 5 are your funnel steps. You can fabricate flat pipes when you characterize your pipe ventures as a different objective.

Utilize a different objective set for your miniaturized scale or ancillary purposes.

Promptly turn off objectives that don't gather information any longer or that are out of date. Later on, you can utilize them to follow other significant site activities. What's more, it will slant your general performance to see if you leave them on.

Set up an alternate view for term and pages/session objectives if you need your general change rate to bode well. High transformation rates for secondary purposes will slant your general objective change rate information.

Notwithstanding session-based objectives, characterize determined measurements so you can set up client change rate objectives also. We talk about this in a moment.

Objectives are session-based. Two visits to your "thank you" page in one session brings about one goal.

"Objectives are critical to examine the presentation of your points of arrival, channels, and so on. An appropriate structure and reasonable naming shows for your objective sets are amazingly useful for you and other individuals that approach a similar revealing perspective."

Set Up Goal Values

It is anything but difficult to increase the value of every one of your exchanges on the off chance that you are running an internet business website. Yet, imagine a scenario where you manage a lead generation or substance site.

Like I referenced previously, every site has its special arrangement of business destinations, KPIs, and objectives. What's more, toward the end, on the off chance that you characterize an activity or result like an objective in Google Analytics, it ought to contain a specific worth.

Here are two models:

Lead generation site

100 leads in a year, total income from those leads is $10000. This implies revenue per lead rises to $100. On the off chance that you set an objective in Google Analytics on the "thank you" page after somebody presents a lead structure, you need to include an objective estimation of $100.

Content site

1000 supporters are worth $50000 income in a year. The pay per supporter (on a yearly premise) rises to

$50. So the objective estimation of another endorser is $50 (determined with LTV of one year).

These are two straightforward instances of how to decide the objective incentive for explicit activities on your site.

Remember:

Try not to set an objective incentive on the "thank you page" of a web-based business exchange. You, as of now, measure the estimation of web-based business exchange in the event that you set up internet business following on your site (which I exceptionally suggest).

Work with relative objective qualities if you don't have the foggiest idea of how to set an exact incentive for the activities on your site. This is no issue by any stretch of the imagination since you can upgrade on these relative numbers too. What's more, in the event that you know the estimation of your large scale objective, you can characterize comparable qualities to your different goals.

Defining up objective qualities enables you to more readily investigate your substance viability by a measurement called "page esteem." It gives you how significant your page is in connection to the Google Analytics objectives. Should you need to go from extraordinary to marvelous, I prescribe to look at this helpful guide on Online Behavior also. It discusses page speed, something you can break down in setting to page worth and objectives.

Make User Level Calculated Metrics

99% of the reports in Google Analytics are session-based. As I would see it, you should see client level measurements also.

Here is a model (internet business site):

- Pete visits your website on January first and perspectives two-item pages.

- Pete returns on January third and adds one item to his bin however doesn't change over.

- Pete visits the site on January fifth and purchases your item.

On default, Google Analytics measures a session-based transformation rate. For this situation, 33.33%. This number is slanted since Pete is one and a similar individual.

If Pete visits your site multiple times through a similar program and gadget, we can remember him as ONE client. The client-based change rate rises to 100% of all things considered.

Let's be honest, you will never get 100% precise numbers, yet give a valiant effort to get the ideal measurements!

I need you to consider a lot of client-based measurements that work for you.

Portion Goal Metrics

You are going to gather important information on the off chance that you pursue the sketched out strides in this instructional exercise.

How about we accept you have gathered one month of Google Analytics objective information in your Google Analytics account.

Presently it's an ideal opportunity to dissect and enhance these outcomes.

You could begin by examining your general objectives and objective change rates.

Be that as it may, you have to fragment your information in the event that you need to show signs of improvement comprehension of your crowd and diverse objective gatherings.

A few inquiries you might need to reply:

- What is the ROI of my new guests contrasted with returning (steadfast) guests?

- Are you sure geographic locales performing superior to other people?

- Do individuals convert on versatile too?

- Which presentation pages drive the most changes?

- What times of our day are the most beneficial for selling our items?

These are only a couple of instances of powerful inquiries you could answer when segmenting your information.

Five report recommendations to kick you off:

- Area report (Audience >> Geo >> Location)

- Gadget Category report (Audience >> Mobile >> Overview)

- Channels report (Acquisition >> All Traffic >> Channels)

- Points of arrival report (Behavior >> Site Content >> Landing Pages)

- Objective outline report (Conversions >> Goals >> Overview)

You can section your Google Analytics objectives (exclusively or totaled) to practically all measurements that are accessible.

"It's great to realize your normal change rate. It's pleasant to realize your normal change rate for various portions of your site. It's urgent to know where you have to make enhancements dependent on your division results. Be that as it may, everything doesn't have any significance if you don't make a move to really improve your outcomes!"

Go Beyond Google Analytics Interface

It's extraordinary to get a first thought on how your site and channels interact via the Google Analytics interface.

In any case, if you like to crunch your information to concoct increasingly concealed bits of knowledge, the Google Analytics API can genuinely enable you to out.

Here is a short instructional exercise to begin:

Stage 1: Install Google Analytics Sheets Add-on (FREE). You should see an "add-on" menu after you have introduced this element: "Include on"

Refresh the page if you don't see it yet.

Stage 2: Create a New Report.

Click on the "make new report" connection and fill in the measurements and measurements you need to maneuver into Google sheets.

Stage 3: Check Your Sample Report Configuration.

On default, the API chooses the most recent seven days. You can alter this field to your very own needs.

Please note this is just indicating the arrangement of your report and not yet any information.

So as to maneuver any information into Google sheets, you have to tap on "Run reports":

Stage 4: Check Your Report Data.

Also, presently, the information is prepared for you.

You can see:

- The date of when the last report ran, regardless of whether there is sampled information or not.

- View the name that has a place with your report.

- Collected review of your report.

- A breakdown of your report dependent on the measurements and measurements you have chosen.

Stage 5: Manipulate the Data.

This is only the beginning of how you can get precise measurements and measurements maneuvered into Google sheets.

For our situation, you need to work with your Google Analytics objectives.

Here is a complete rundown of measurements and measurements right now accessible by means of the Google Analytics API.

By doing this, you will show signs of improvement comprehension of the potential outcomes of the Google Analytics API.

A snappy model:

You need to get the outright objective numbers in Google sheets for objective number 1.

All things considered, you have to add ga:goal1 Completions to the measurement field.

Interestingly, you can utilize a considerable amount of Excel equations to control the information in an ideal manner.

You should join your objective information with different measurements to figure a worth more in accordance with your KPIs.

The following stages are fabricating a visual around it so you can likely screen the exhibition and discover regions for development.

This short instructional exercise is implied as a beginning stage for utilizing the Google Analytics API.

"The Google Analytics API causes you to computerize your announcing endeavors with the goal that you can invest more energy streamlining your site execution."

Follow up on Your Insights

There is one significant last advance after you have caught essential bits of knowledge from straightforward Google Analytics objective information.

Furthermore, that is following up on the bits of knowledge you found.

A couple of basic models:

Understanding: your email showcasing efforts perform not just as they did before. Activity: discover ways on the most proficient method to improve your email battles.

Knowledge: you have a better than expected surrender rate at pipe stage 3. Activity: utilize subjective studies and client tests to discover progressively regarding why clients desert your site on this progression. Make a theory around it and set up a couple of A/B tests to test your speculation so that you can ideally improve your funnel achievement rate.

Knowledge: returning guests convert 5x superior to your new guests. Activity: set up an appropriate retargeting effort to transform more guests into clients. What's more, attempt to convince all the more first time guests by offering appealing limits for turning into a customer.

So discovering bits of knowledge is exceptionally extraordinary; however, it is tied in with making a move.

"Many individuals discover that something isn't right on their site, yet you can possibly get more cash-flow on the off chance that you realize how to fix it and do as such."

Here are things you should consider when defining up objectives in Google Analytics:

- Adopting a vital strategy when defining up your goals requires some investment; however, it's very justified, despite all the trouble.

- Start with an estimation and usage plan before you permanently add a couple of objectives to your Google Analytics see. You should utilize a spreadsheet to illustrate your goals.

- Google Analytics objectives are session-based; consider client level objective measurements also.

- Remember that each revealing perspective has a point of confinement of four objectives defines five objectives for every set.

- Google Analytics objectives don't work retroactively.

- Objectives are just checked once per session.

- Typical articulations prove to be useful when defining up your objectives.

- Confirm your objective before actualizing it (in light of verifiable information).

- Set up funnels for plainly characterized ways on your site.

- Include objective qualities for every one of your objectives (a particular case is an online business "thank you" page).

- Utilize the API to haul objective information out of Google Analytics.

- Be cautious when you measure over various areas.

- Utilize an external duplicate/glue device to duplicate objectives, starting with one view then onto the next.

- Set up occasion, put together objectives for significant with respect to page associations.

- Investigate span and pages/session objectives in a setting of increasingly essential goals on your site.

- You can make an objective dormant or replace it; however, you can't erase it.

- Use objective portrayals that anyone can get it.

- Setting funnel stage 1 as required influences the channel report itself.

- At the point when you set up objectives, there may be a short postponement before they really work.

- Include an explanation at whatever point you add or change an objective.

Chapter Seven

Data Collection and Analysis

Having a site that is improved for versatility is fundamentally significant. An ongoing report by Pew Internet uncovers that 56% of grown-ups in the US have cell phones and more than 33% claim tablets. You can utilize Google Analytics to help reveal information about how your site is performing for your versatile clients.

At the point when you see your dashboard:

Click "Audience"

Choose "Mobile"

Click on "Devices"

This pulls up a diagram that uncovers some necessary data about how mobile clients are utilizing your site. You can follow everything from Engagements, to Visits, to Bounce rate, and Which cell phone your crowd used to get to your site

If you are keen on perceiving how mobile clients are reacting to your website, audit two specific metrics:

1. Contrast Your Bounce Rate with those for Mobile Users

Are the rates about the equivalent, or are those from portable clients higher? If you see that bounce rates are raised among clients on cell phones, it might be an excellent opportunity to take a look at your mobile procedure. Set aside the effort to assess how your site looks on various cell phones and tablets. Offer your discoveries with an expert website specialist when you're examining how you can improve the webpage experience for mobile clients.

2. Assess the Bounce Rates by Specific Device Users

This will help give some important knowledge into how your site is performing on certain cell phones and tablets. If bounce rates are higher for a particular gadget, it's important that you figure out how to get to one of those gadgets to investigate your site. Odds are there's presumably an issue with how it's rendering for those specific gadget clients.

Another significant thing to remember is that Google has, as of late, emphasized the significance of mobile improvement with regards to their internet searcher rankings. So you'll need to ensure your site renders well crosswise over various gadgets.

Look at User Behavior of Specific Segments

Everybody who visits your site matters to your business. Be that as it may, it's essential that site proprietors focus on the estimation of specific clients. For instance, possibly, you're running a PPC (pay per click) crusade for your business, and each snap costs you cash. It's particularly essential to comprehend the viability of your battle and track those changes.

So as to get down into the bare essential of your site's client conduct, you can utilize the Google Analytics progress dividing instrument to follow how your clients are getting to your website and whether they are making the ideal move.

It's anything but difficult to begin following this:

Click "Audience"

Choose "Advanced Segments" (It should give you the alternative to choose various choices.)

Choose "Paid Search Traffic"

Choose "Non-Paid Search Traffic"

Choose "Direct Traffic"

Choose "Referral Traffic"

Click "Apply"

You would now be able to see information for specific traffic measurements of site guests. This enables you to monitor things like your PPC surrender rates and adjust your crusades to help meet your business objectives. Or on the other hand, if you see that you are getting high volumes of referral traffic, consider composing a couple focused on visitor presents on help draw in progressively potential clients. Set aside the effort to do a more profound plunge into Advanced Segmentation.

You can likewise look at significant territories over your site, for example,

Ecommerce Statistics

Are you selling things on your website? Provided that this is true, this merits a look. It can furnish you with better learning of who your clients are.

Set Goals

You additionally have the choice of making objectives channels inside GA. Objectives channels let you track how your site guests are changing over. For instance, regardless of whether they download your white papers or sign up for your newsletter.

Wellsprings of Traffic

How are the behaviors of mobile clients on your site? Contrast this with desktop clients. Utilize this data to help plan your mobile procedure pushing ahead.

Don't merely stop with the essential statistics if you need to comprehend guest conduct genuinely. An in-depth look will assist you with fitting your site to address the issues of various clients.

Make Stronger CTAs via In-Page Analytics

Convincing invitations to take action helps to improve your business conversions. What's more, it isn't only your copy you should focus on; it's your site configuration also. If you want to improve your invitations to take action, why not attempt some A/B testing?

Basically, you make two styles of a page with a little distinction. Possibly it's a button with a particular source of inspiration, and you plan one in blue and one in red. Test them out to figure out which rendition improves your sales. Split testing is exceptionally successful, yet can likewise be tedious.

GA's In-Page Analytics highlight gives you a chance to see the landing pages that convert best. It tracks click rates on various pages. You can likewise utilize it to see how near you are to reaching explicit site objectives. The report is both wealthy in information and exceptionally visual. Site owners can use this element to respond to critical inquiries, for example,

- Are guests reacting to your CTAs?

- Does your site configuration direct people to critical substances?

- What do guests click on when they look at your site?

- Does your site have an interruption – perhaps a live chat or pop-up feature – that is hindering valuable content?

- Which menu things are most much of the time clicked by guests?

The In-Page Analytics highlight additionally gives you a chance to comprehend what is "above the fold." Popular in the paper business, this references what your guests see when they arrive on your site. Are you utilizing this territory to grandstand your most important content? To discover, click on "Browser Size" in the center menu bar while using the In-Page feature.

Data Analytics

As the way toward dissecting raw information to discover patterns and answer questions, the meaning of information investigation catches its expansive extent of the field. In any case, it incorporates numerous methods with various objectives.

The data analytics procedure has some key segments that are required for any activity. By consolidating these parts, a productive data analytics activity will give a clear picture of where you are, the place you have been, and where you ought to go.

- By and large, this procedure starts with a spellbinding examination. This is the way toward depicting verifiable patterns in information. Unmistakable analysis expects to respond to the inquiry, "what occurred?" This frequently includes estimating customary pointers, for example, return on investment (ROI). The tips utilized will be distinctive for every industry. Descriptive analytics doesn't settle on forecasts or legitimately inform choices. It centers around abridging information in a meaningful and expressive manner.

- The following essential piece of information examination is progressed investigation. This picce of information science exploits propelled devices to remove information, make expectations, and find patterns. These tools incorporate old-style measurements just as AI. AI advances, for example, neural systems, regular language handling, assessment examination, and increasingly empower progressed investigation. This data gives new knowledge from information. Progressed examination addresses "what if?" questions.

- The accessibility of AI strategies, extensive informational collections, and modest figuring force has empowered the utilization of these systems in numerous businesses. The accumulation of substantial informational collections is instrumental in allowing these procedures. Massive information analytics will enable organizations to reach meaningful inferences from mind-boggling and changed information sources, which has made conceivable by propels in parallel preparing and modest computational power.

How Analytics Work

The initial step for each data science undertaking is data accumulation, i.e, getting the real raw information.

There are two different ways to do this:

A) You can pick at least one "smart tool" to utilize. These services will gather the information for you consequently. You need to copy and paste a scrap of code into your site, and you are all set. (For example, Hotjar, Google Analytics, CrazyEgg Google Optimize, and so on.)

B) You can gather the data yourself. (For example, employing a javascript code scrap that sends information to a .csv plain content document on your server.) It's harder to actualize since it requires some coding abilities. In any case, in the long term, this arrangement will serve you much better (and it will be progressively beneficial, as well) than rendition A.

Why? Here's a list:

- You'll have your information – you won't rely upon Hotjar, Google Analytics, and so forth.

- You'll have one bound together information stockroom — no requirement for incorporations, API hacks, etc.

- There won't be any confinements on how you can utilize your information or how you can interface various data points. (For example, you can't use your raw data in Google Analytics to execute AI models; however, you can do it on the off chance that you have your very own database.)

- You can confide in your information 100%. (Not any more secret elements. You know your information since you claim it.)

- Information server expenses are fundamentally lower than outsider apparatuses' month to month charges.

- Whichever way you pick, it merits seeing how crude information gathering functions all in all — and how you can gather information from your site guests' conduct.

- Do it for yourself or utilizing an outsider apparatus fundamentally the same as things are occurring in the engine!

- How does information gathering work?

- How about we go with the least complex model!

You have a site, and you might want to gather each guest mouse click for a forthcoming information science venture.

How would you do that?

Initially, execute a following undetectable content (otherwise known as "information accumulation content") on each interactive component of your site! Starting there on, when a site guest taps on a particular part (for example a connection or a catch), the snap makes two things occur:

- The button will do what it ought to do. For instance, it will arrive at the client on the page she clicked.

- The data collection content will send a little information bundle to your information stockroom.

As straightforward as that.

You could follow each client collaboration (how about we call them "occasions") on your site (or in your mobile application): site visits, highlight utilization, taps, clicks — even mouse movements if you have to.

Instructions to store the gathered raw data

At the point when the collected raw data hits your information distribution center, it tends to be put away in various arrangements.

For new companies, the best configuration is the plain content arrangement, as it is truly adaptable. You can envision this as a basic .txt, .csv or .tsv record with content in it. Numerous organizations use this model.

But on the other hand, it merits referencing that numerous different organizations (for example, practically all worldwide organizations) like to gather their information legitimately into SQL databases (or to other comparative organized arrangements).

Furthermore, there are a few different approaches to store your information. (Diagram databases, NoSQL databases, and so forth.)

In this model, I'll keep it basic and will go with the most widely recognized arrangement: everyday content organization.

Keep in mind that every occasion from a site guest (for example, a tick on your site) makes one line of information utilizing your recently actualized data collection contents. This line goes into a document on your information server. We consider this record with a lot of occasions in it a log. You can have more than one log, yet practically every one of them will have a similar format.

What sort of raw data would it be advisable for you to gather?

If you maintain an online business, you can gather and store a virtually limitless measure of information.

This brings up the undeniable issue: what you should gather and what you shouldn't.

The standard here is straightforward: gather all that you can. Each snap, each site hit, each component utilization, everything.

It's fascinating to take note of that (as per showcase benchmarks), most new businesses who pursue this gather everything-rule wind up utilizing under 10% of their information. Their information researchers don't move 90%!

So for what reason do they gather everything? The appropriate response is: because you can never comprehend what information you will require later on for your information ventures.

Suppose you need to change a crucial 3-year-old component of your online item. You would prefer not to wreck anything, so before the change, you will invest some energy to comprehend the right job of that crucial 3-year-old element. For that, you should break down your information reflectively. Challenges, you understand that you didn't gather any information about it. Game over, you've quite recently lost 3-years' worth of data. Get it?

If you start considering gathering a particular information moment that it's required for an information science venture, you are now past the point of no return.

What's more, that is the explanation for the guideline "gather all that you can."

What sort of data would it be advisable for you not to gather?

There are some conspicuous confinements.

Yet, the cost of putting away information isn't one of those. Putting away information (in the cloud at any rate) is modest today.

The genuine impediments are:

1. Engineering time: The engineers need to invest energy to actualize the following contents. Also, if you have a mind-boggling information distribution center, you will require a full-time individual to manufacture and keep up the information foundation, as well. So if your engineers invest more energy gathering crude information than executing

new highlights, fixes, or plan thoughts, at that point, perhaps you are to the information center.

2. Good judgment: indeed, regardless of whether it's modest, you can, in any case, over-burden your database if you accomplish silly things. For example, if you log each mouse development of each client each millisecond. You ought not to do that.

3. Neglected to-consider it: as a rule, the principle motivation behind why individuals don't gather specific information focuses is that they mostly overlook that they ought to be collected. It occurs, don't stress. If you need to stay away from it, I prescribe setting up a workshop in which you sit together and talk through how and what information to gather and why. I expounded more on that in this article.

4. Legitimate questions: You ought to consider lawful inquiries, as well. They vary from nation to nation, so I prescribe counseling with a legal expert in your country.

Furthermore, one more celebrated remark here. A few nations have exacting lawful confinements about data collection; others don't. Despite the guidelines: consistently think about morals. Never gather information from your site guests that you wouldn't need to be collected about you.

This is how raw data accumulation works at a significant level. Google Analytics, Mixpanel, Crazyegg, or your very own information distribution centers — all depend on these standards. There are little contrasts, yet now you comprehend what occurs out of sight, and you can be progressively sure when discussing data accumulation with your associates.

Mindset for Science Data Business

The objective of information accumulation is to improve the nature of the item or administration and not to produce more benefits? This doesn't imply that you won't get more cash-flow as a result of your information science ventures. I instead need to feature the needs.

On a significant level, you can accomplish two things with information science.

1. Understanding your group of spectators better. Finding out about their needs, their battles, their inspirations, their habits, and their connections to your item or administration.

2. Using this comprehension to make a superior item or administration and transforming that into the benefit.

The request is significant.

Your primary need ought to be to support your clients. As a result of that, your item or administration will thrive. What's more, that better item or administration will bring you more clients, additionally returning clients and in the long run, more income.

Business information science the attitude

The business information science attitude

Data Science Project Steps

At its center, (pretty much) every data venture assumes a similar role in your business. Data science causes you to make simpler, quicker, and better choices.

As straightforward as it sounds as confounded, it can get, in actuality.

How about we investigate the ordinary six stages of a data science venture:

- Data Collection
- Data Storage
- Data Cleaning
- Data Analysis
- Correspondence, Data representation
- Data-driven Decision

Each step has its difficulties. We should go through them individually so I can show you the significant challenges you ought to know about at each progression – to avoid or solve them.

Data Collection – were numerous organizations bomb

"Trash in, trash out." – As the essential data rule says. What's more, it's valid.

Such a large number of information ventures come up short at this simple initial step. Such a large number of organizations gather fragmented, untrustworthy information, and all that they do after that is failed.

True story from a genuine organization: we were doing an A/B test as the last period of a 2-month extensive examination. It was a mind-boggling test, with many channel steps and site pages included. It ought to have run for 30 days to gather enough information that focuses on a measurably noteworthy outcome.

The main issue was that around the end of the second seven-day stretch of the examination, a naturally enlisted junior designer expelled one of our tracking codes from one of the website pages we tried.

The fact of the matter is: we understood uniquely toward the finish of the 30-day trial that the code was expelled. Even though it was just a single minor subpage (the issue caused an expected ~5-10% information error), we needed to waste the entire A/B testing venture and restart it from the very first moment since half of the analysis depended on slanted information.

The most exceedingly awful thing in this story was not unreasonably. We needed to re-run an A/B test – however, that we would never confide in our information again. We generally needed to double-check and significantly increased check everything before we made ends. What's more, that backed us off for a considerable length of time.

The lesson of the story is: appropriate following, and information accumulation is critical for each business doing information science. My particular proposal is to have in any event one individual in your group who's liable for information gathering and who twofold checks everything to do with it in any event once per month.

What to gather? It depends, but the general idea is to gather all that you can because information stockpiling is moderately modest these days.

In any case, you need to remember that the more things you track on your site:

- the more engineering time you ought to apportion to execute and look after following

- the slower your website or application will be (we are discussing microseconds here – however it can add effectively)

- the more mind-boggling your information foundation becomes

- etc.

Data Storage and Cleaning

Data storage and cleaning are the duty of data engineers. It's an exceptionally specialized activity, yet, as a rule, you don't need to stress over it to an extreme. Not unreasonably, it's insignificant or straightforward. It's merely that it's a well-characterized work, so when you procure a (decent) information engineer, she will know precisely how to deal with this piece of your information business. There are not very numerous traps. Furthermore, a significant part of it tends to be computerized, so it's hugely advantageous.

Data Analysis – removing esteem

This is the place business information science gets energizing – for agents in any event.

A data expert is an artist. She gets a square of information, and afterward, she cuts and cuts until she gets something genuinely extraordinary.

Also, it's an innovative procedure.

I'm an information expert on the most fundamental level, and I know as a matter of fact that when you have a sea of information before you, it tends to be extremely scary.

Regularly, you don't have a clue where to begin.

In any case, there are a couple of rules that can help. Here are the best three that helped me:

1. Great questions.

To find helpful solutions, you need to ask the correct inquiries. That usually originates from the administration (or different associates), who, as of now, have doubts dependent on their experience.

For this situation, an information expert's essential employment is to demonstrate or invalidate these doubts (how about we call them speculations).

Note: A typical doubt is that refuting speculation is a stage in reverse. Individuals are taking a gander at it as the disappointment of a thought. That's an inappropriate attitude, however. At the point when a decent information investigator demonstrates or refutes an idea, she finds numerous new things all through the procedure, so she can offer at least one elective arrangement that is superior to the first thought.

Let me additionally underline the positive qualities in the expression "great inquiry." Answering awful addresses interferes with an information venture fundamentally. Terrible questions can be:

- Irrelevant questions ("What occurs if we change the logo size by one pixel?")

- Questions that aren't business-related.

- Ambiguous questions ("How do individuals like us?")

- Or on the other questions that we don't (and won't) have information to reply.

2. Qualitative examination.

There is nothing like seeing a genuine client communicating with your item. Observing only 5-6 UX tests will give you at any rate 10-20 thoughts for where to begin your data venture.

3. Best practices.

It indeed relies upon the given information venture and on the particular business use case.

Business Analytics Today

Should you start with data science for your business today, I'd suggest concentrating on one specific thing before you do whatever else.

That is discovering your single most significant measurement.

You'll discover the same numbers of names for this as there are books regarding the matter:

- OMTM – One Metric That Matters

- WIG – Wildly Important Goal (by McChesney and Covey)

- North Star Metric (via Sean Ellis)

And so forth.

Various names, same point You need to make sense of your single most significant measurement.

What's more, you should put this measurement over each other metric you have — measure it and keep it as your primary core interest.

A decent most significant measurement is:

- Basic (so everybody at your organization comprehends it right away)

- Quantifiable (so it's a genuine number)

176

- Depicting your business objectives truly well (so it matters)

what's more,

There is just one of them! (Indeed, I know, it's elusive one measurement. Be that as it may, it's conceivable — and once you have it, it will be precious!)

How about we take the least complicated model: a developed web-based business.

What makes the best number one essential measurement for an online web-based business that has been working for over ten years?

It's income! Why? It's basic. (Benefit, for example, would be a lot harder to figure and comprehend for everybody at your organization.) It's anything but difficult to gauge. It ponders the organization's business objectives. Also, it's one single measurement. Great.

The circumstance is straightforward for full-grown web based business organizations. At different organizations (for example, early-stage new companies, progressively complex plans of action, and so on.), it tends to be a lot harder to make sense of it.

Data Communications

This is where most data science tasks come up short.

Fascinating, would you say it isn't?

You can be the best examiner working with the best informational index on the planet. But if you can't impart your discoveries proficiently, you will have zero effect.

That is the bad dream of each data proficient.

There are many barricades here. Also, I've seen every one of them: information doubter (or fundamentally moronic) associates, over-confounded introductions, vague outlines.

The truth of the matter is that everybody at your organization should be engaged with a request to fabricate a culture where individuals can impart and utilize information.

I have two specific proposals for you:

1. Instruct!

Information experts should hold introductions consistently – about their ongoing discoveries as well as regarding why information science is significant for the organization. Start with things like what an information investigator does, how the information science business works, how partners can assemble self-serving information answers for themselves, etc.

Representatives ought to teach data researchers, also. They should assist them with creating and convey better introductions.

2. Keep it straightforward.

Everything about your correspondence ought to be as necessary as it tends to be!

No extravagant logical words (you would prefer not to flaunt),

No confounded diagrams (you don't need to show everything),

No interminable messages (you need individuals to peruse what you compose).

If you can show your information-driven takeaways in a single line diagram and clarify them in one sentence, you ought to do it. Everybody will be glad about it.

Data-Driven Decision Making

Have you, at any point, heard the abbreviation "HIPPO"?

It represents the most generously compensated individual's feelings, and it was an entrenched business basic leadership technique for a considerable length of time.

On account of data science, it's not the case any longer.

Notwithstanding, few out of every odd chief is prepared for this to change. Indeed, even a very first-rate information undertaking can (and will) fall flat now, since you hurt somebody's sentiments or sense of self. I know this sounds awful; however, this is the awkward truth. (Particularly at more prominent organizations with 500+ representatives.)

You can counteract this by setting up a data-driven organization culture at a convenient time. (I more often than not prescribe to begin to consider your information technique when you have 10-50 representatives.)

At a higher organization, it will be exponentially harder to make your association information-driven.

It's additionally critical to send your directors to information workshops and ensure that they build up the correct outlook.

Three Major Data Science Applications

There is such a vast number of chances to transform your information into value.

All the more explicitly, at online organizations, these are the three most regular reasonable uses of information science:

Business Analytics (Descriptive Analytics)

It responds to the inquiries of "what has occurred previously?" and "where are we now?"

(For example, announcing, estimating maintenance, finding the correct client fragments, pipe examination, and so on.)

Predictive Analytics

It responds to the inquiry, "what will occur later on?"

(For example, early cautioning (foreseeing which client will drop her membership one month from now), anticipating the showcasing spending you will require in the next quarter, and so forth.)

Data-Based Product

An item that works utilizing your recorded information. (For example, self-learning chatbots, suggestion frameworks, picture acknowledgment, voice acknowledgment, and so on.)

Which out of them brings the most business value?

To answer this question, your keyword is: ROI – Return on Investment.

From a purely business approach, data science is an investment of your resources, and you want to have some return on it.

Question is: which of the three projects above brings the most significant value for your business right now?

Business analytics? Predictive Analytics? Or are you creating a data-based product?

It is an open question and one to which only you know the answer. But here's a typical pattern I see from my clients all the time.

Everyone is excited about machine learning, predictive analytics, and data-based products (like chatbots). Yet, many of these companies:

- Do not have a clear funnel (that they measure step-by-step)

- Do not know too much about their key metrics (not to speak of their most important metric),

- Do not have precise numbers on their most significant user segments

Sometimes they do not even know the number of users (or paying users) they have. These are all Descriptive analytics and business analytic questions.

Until you get the answer to these questions (and other essential but straightforward business inquiries), you shouldn't go for AI projects.

If you know yourself, my strong recommendation is: invest in simple reports and business analytics first. By knowing the basics, you will create tremendous business value: you will see more clearly, and you will understand your audience better.

Perhaps by learning your audience's wants, you will map out a user-need for an image recognition system in your product, and in a few months (when the business data science fundamentals are already set), you can start to work on that, too.

Calculate the return on investment, and go for the more straightforward data science projects first.

Types of Data Analytics

Data analytics is a vast field. There are four essential kinds of information examination: diagnostic, descriptive, prescriptive, and predictive analytics. Each type has an alternate objective and a better place in the data analysis process. These are likewise essential information investigation applications in business.

- Descriptive analytics helps answer inquiries regarding what occurred. These strategies condense massive datasets to depict results to partners. By creating key performance indicators (KPIs), these techniques can help track victories or disappointments. Measurements, for example, return on investment (ROI), are utilized in numerous businesses. Particular metrics are created to follow execution in specific companies. This procedure requires the collection of vital information, handling of the information, data visualization, and analysis. This procedure gives basic knowledge into past performance.

- Diagnostic analytics helps answer inquiries concerning why things occurred. These systems supplement progressively fundamental illustrative examination. They take the discoveries from distinct investigation and burrow further to discover the reason. The exhibition markers are additionally researched to find why they showed signs of improvement or more terrible. This, by and large, happens in three stages:

o Distinguish irregularities in the information. These might be sudden changes in measurement or a specific market.

o Information that is identified with these oddities is gathered.

o Factual procedures are utilized to discover connections and patterns that clarify these abnormalities.

• Predictive analytics helps answer inquiries regarding what will occur later on. These systems utilize chronicled information to distinguish inclines and decide whether they are probably going to repeat. Prescient analytical instruments give a significant understanding of what may occur later on, and its systems incorporate an assortment of factual and AI procedures, for example, neural networks, choice trees, and relapse.

- Prescriptive analytics helps answer inquiries regarding what ought to be finished. By utilizing bits of knowledge from the prescient examination, information-driven choices can be made. This enables organizations to settle on educated decisions in the face regarding vulnerability. Prescriptive analytic methods depend on AI methodologies that can discover designs in enormous datasets. By examining past choices and occasions, the probability of different results can be evaluated.

These kinds of information investigation give the understanding that organizations need to settle on viable and effective choices. Utilized in the blend, they provide a balanced comprehension of an organization's needs and openings.

Role of Data Analysts

Data analysts exist at the crossing point of information technology, business, and statistics. They join these fields so as to support organizations and associations to succeed. The essential objective of a data analyst is to expand proficiency and improve execution by finding patterns in information.

Crafts of a data analyst include working with information all through the analysis pipeline. This implies working with information in different manners. The essential strides in the information investigation procedure are data mining, managing, statistical analysis, and presentation. The significance and balance of these means rely upon the information being utilized and the objective of the investigation.

Data mining is a necessary procedure for some data analytics undertakings. This includes removing information from unstructured information sources. These may incorporate written content, enormous, complex databases, or raw sensor information. The fundamental strides in this procedure are to remove, change, and load data (regularly called ETL.) These means convert raw data into an accessible and sensible format. This gets information ready for analysis and storage. Data mining is commonly the most time-escalated step in the analysis pipeline.

Data management or warehousing is another crucial part of an analyst's job. Data warehousing includes planning and implementing databases that enable simple access to the outcome of data mining. This progression, for the most part, includes making and overseeing SQL databases. Non-relational and NoSQL databases are winding up progressively healthy too.

Statistical analysis is the core of data analytics. This is the manner by which the bits of knowledge are made from data. The two statistics and AI methods are utilized to examine information. Vast information is used to create statistical models that uncover data trends. These models would then be able to be applied to new information to settle on expectations and advise essential leadership. Statistical programming dialects, for example, R or Python (with pandas), are fundamental to this procedure. Furthermore, open-source libraries and bundles, for example, TensorFlow, empower advanced examination.

The last step in numerous data analytics procedures is data presentation. This is a fundamental step that enables bits of knowledge to be imparted to partners. Data visualization is regularly the most significant device in data presentation. Impressive displays are necessary to recount the story in the information which may support administrators and directors to comprehend the significance of these bits of knowledge.

Importance of Data Analytics

The uses of data analytics are extensive. Analyzing enormous information can streamline proficiency in a wide range of businesses. Improving execution empowers organizations to prevail in an inexorably competitive world. Data analytics is being utilized with extraordinary achievement in various fields.

Perhaps the earliest adopter is the money related sector. Data analytics has a tremendous job in the banking and fund enterprises, used to anticipate market patterns, and evaluate risk. FICO ratings are a case of data analytics that influences everybody. These scores utilize numerous data points to decide to loan risk. Data analytics is likewise used to identify and counteract fraud to improve productivity and decrease the risk for commercial organizations.

The utilization of data analytics goes past boosting benefits and ROI, be that as it may. Data analytics can give necessary data to health services (health informatics), prevention of crime, and ecological security. These utilizations of data analytics utilize these procedures to improve the world.

In spite of the fact that data analysis and statistics have consistently been utilized in scientific research, progressed analytic methods and vast information take into account numerous new bits of knowledge. These procedures can discover trends in complex frameworks. Researchers are, as of now, utilizing AI to ensure natural life.

The utilization of data analytics in social insurance is now far-reaching. Foreseeing persistent results, productively designating funding, and improving indicative procedures are only a couple of instances of how data analytics is changing medicinal services. The pharmaceutical business is likewise being altered by AI. Drug discovery is an unpredictable errand with numerous factors. AI can incredibly improve tranquilize disclosure. Pharmaceutical organizations additionally use information examination to comprehend the market for drugs and foresee their deals.

The web of things (IoT) is a field that is detonating close by AI. These gadgets give an incredible chance for data analytics. IoT gadgets frequently contain numerous sensors that gather essential information points for their activity. Devices like the Nest indoor regulator track development and temperature to direct warming and cooling. Savvy devices like this can utilize information to gain from and foresee your conduct. This will give advance home computerization that can adjust to the manner in which you live.

The utilization of data analytics is apparently interminable. An ever-increasing number of information is being gathered each day — this presents new chances to apply data analytics to more pieces of business, science, and regular daily existence.

Chapter Eight

Free Resources for Google Analytics

Google Analytics isn't, in every case, simple to learn.

Truth be told, it's entangled to the point that numerous individuals disregard it – a significant misstep. On the off chance that you spend a considerable bit of your day, consistently, tweaking your site and improving it for web search tools, guests, and deals, at that point, doesn't it bode well to ensure you're getting the most value for your money? How would you break down what you're doing?

The issue with Google Analytics is that it resembles learning another game, for example, surfing – when you first stand up on a surfboard you're similar to "yippee I can surf now!" however then you understand getting past the fundamentals of riding the whitewater is a lofty expectation to absorb information. It's effortless to sign in to Google

Analytics and see what your traffic was for as far back as 30 days. It's significantly harder to make sense of how to break down is by geo, traffic source, page classification, and so forth.

Google Analytics is gigantically incredible, and keeping in mind that there's not a viable replacement for signing in and investing energy with it, the accompanying assets will help get you up to speed quicker.

Google Analytics Academy

Directly from Google themselves, Google Analytics Academy will walk you through a progression of self-guided courses and exercises where you gain from the specialists. You can test your insight and join the learning network in an intelligent discussion where you can learn from your companions. What better spot to take in Google Analytics than from the creators themselves? Their courses incorporate Google Tag Manager Fundamentals, Mobile App Analytics Fundamentals, E-Commerce Analytics: from Data to Decisions, Google Analytics Platform Principles, and Digital Analytics Fundamentals.

After you feel that you've adapted everything, you can take one of their certification tests.

Moz

Moz is maybe the headteacher of the majority on inbound promoting and SEO that likewise sells programming. Their devotion to teaching us is exceptional. On their blog, Kristi Hines strolls you through an itemized arrangement installation of Google Analytics. Kristi clarifies what it is and how to utilize it to further your potential benefit. It is finished with applicable pictures that walk you through each part of Google Analytics from the following instruments to online store settings with your WordPress site. It is intended for the amateur who thinks nothing about Google Analytics. It will take you from a total beginner to a power client in a few minutes.

Google Analytics Training and Certification

Google takes it a stride further with Google Analytics Training and Certifications. Here, they give to the Google Analytics Academy you see over, an arrangement agenda, a begin direct, an assistance focus, and a testing focus. With the expansion of workshops and recordings including introduction, moderate, and propelled courses, you may locate a confirmed coach in your general vicinity to learn face to face.

They additionally offer links on their YouTube channel for the individuals who adapt best with videos.

Analytics Talk

In spite of the fact that this blog of his hasn't been refreshed in for a short time, there's some ageless gold that makes it still one of the top blogs on analytics on the planet.

They made their whole site around Google Analytics. They offer a few useful blog entries to show you Google Analytics as well as to stay up with the latest with anything new. To give you an example of what they offer, their initial three blog entries were:

1. Understanding the Google Analytics Cohort Report

2. Using Off-Line and Online Data to Drive Google Analytics Remarketing

3. Understanding Cross-Device Measurement and User ID.

These are blog entries intended to keep you at the cutting edge of what's going on with Google Analytics.

Occam's Razor

Avinash Kaushik is most likely the best all-around author on Analytics. He is a Google guy; however, he isn't advancing Google's items constantly. He knows there is a great deal of big business analytics system out there that go past Google Analytics, so he's taking a look at the full range. His mystery sauce is his capacity to take immense, unusual thoughts and distill them down. He addresses all channels of digital marketing to dissect the viability of every one of them and point you the correct way.

The best thing about his write-ups is that he will give you his assessment and guide you. He can be nonpartisan on certain occasions, and exceptionally stubborn in others. Be that as it may that is the thing that starting to intermediates need, clear heading from the aces. Fortunately, he posts about once every month.

The guide on his blog takes you from somebody who has no learning of Google Analytics to somebody who is capable of Google Analytics. He spreads it out in five simple advances: (1) make sense of the ideal vocation way for you, (2) take your first two web analytics device, (3) get taught, (4) play in reality, and (5) secure your first analytics job. When you get the opportunity to stage five, you will have been managing this blog entry for 3 to a half year. It isn't something you adapt overnight on the grounds that there's a great deal of data to take in.

Portent's Interactive Analytics

Ian Laurie is perhaps the most amusing author in the computerized promoting world. What's more, his group has slashes as one of the top web promoting organizations. So you can expect their examination blog entries to be both enlightening and here and there interesting. The group talks at the senior advanced showcasing meetings, so you realize their posts are first class.

Portent's blog and aides are frequently obstinate and energetic. In the event that you need to get some training in an all the more intriguing and propelled way, add their site to your understanding rundown.

A few blasts from the past are the Install Video Guide and Basic Stats Video Guide.

A few people adapt better with videos. They get this, so they made several recordings for those visual students out there. Videos can place more information in a shorter period—hope to pause the video as you take in the report.

The subsequent video following the "introduce video guide" experiences the metrics that they call necessary details. It's always helpful to have paper and pen nearby to record information. Watch right through from the outset and afterward watch it

199

again, recording the essential data that you have to know and how to read and comprehend the details of Google Analytics.